Outshine

An Ovarian Cancer Memoir

KAREN INGALLS

D1153797

ISBN: 978-1-59298-462-6

Library of Congress Catalog Number: 2012902333

Book design and typesetting: Jill Blumer

Printed in the United States of America

First Printing: 2012

16   15   14   13   12   5   4   3   2   1

BEAVER'S POND
PRESS

7108 Ohms Lane
Edina, Minnesota 55439
(952) 829-8818
www.BeaversPondPress.com

To order, visit www.BeaversPondBooks.com or call 1-800-901-3480. Reseller and special sales discounts are available.

To my husband, Jim

Acknowledgments

My deepest gratitude to my grandmother and to my adopted aunt, who inspired and taught me about life and spirituality; thanks to Jill Blumer for sharing her gifts of creativity and art; to Dara Beevas, Amy Quale, and Angela Wiechmann, who believed in, supported, and guided me.

Contents

Prologue

I had gained a few pounds and developed a protruding stomach, both of which were unusual for me. From childhood through my early forties, I was actually underweight, and I drank high-protein drinks in an attempt to gain weight. Once I started menopause, I gained some weight and was in the normal weight range for my age and height. When my weight continued to increase and I could not wear my size 6 slacks, I began an aggressive weight-loss program with Weight Watchers and exercise. I never considered those physical changes to be anything more than normal postmenopausal aging.

❧

Ovarian cancer is the ninth-most common female cancer, and it ranks fifth in cancer deaths among women. Statistically per capita, the mortality rate is 70 percent, versus 15 percent for breast cancer. If diagnosed and treated in Stage I, women have a five-year survival rate of 93 percent. I was Stage II and was initially given a 50 percent survival rate.

Ovarian cancer was once called the "silent killer," because with its vague symptoms, it's usually not diagnosed until Stage III or IV. But at the Minnesota Ovarian Cancer Alliance's twelfth-annual Walk/Run for Ovarian Cancer, I heard the chant "Silent no more." I wore a teal T-shirt with those same words. Because women and physicians are more aware of this disease and its symptoms, ovarian cancer is no longer the silent killer, but it still whispers its presence. I wrote this book in hopes of perking up the ears of women and their partners so they can better hear these whispers. A woman is her own best advocate and knows her body better than anyone, so it's vital that she stay informed and educated.

A bloating or painful abdomen, unexplained weight gain, constipation, or urinary difficulties are some of the common whispering symptoms, but they are also associated with many other ailments or disorders from the benign to the very serious. The *persistence* of these symptoms is the key to detecting ovarian cancer. However, the question for many women is, what's "persistent" in any given time frame? Not every woman has a family history to alert her and her physician to the possibility of ovarian cancer. So, if a woman has any of these symptoms, it is important to get them checked out immediately. Early detection is vital to survival. If a doctor does not consider the possibility of ovarian cancer, I encourage the woman to go to a gynecological oncologist who will have the tests, experience, and expertise to better evaluate the presenting symptoms.

I always felt I was at high risk for developing cancer, because a number of my family members have had different types of the disease. My mother died of stomach cancer at the age of sixty-nine, her sister died of breast cancer while in her early forties, and their brother died of jaw cancer secondary to smoking when he was in his sixties. My paternal great-grandfather died of colon cancer. The family history of breast and colon cancers increased my risk of developing ovarian cancer. After my diagnosis, I pursued genetic counseling and was tested for the *BRCA1* and *BRCA2* genes. These mutated genes have occurred in families with several cases of breast cancer. There's also a higher risk of developing ovarian cancer for women with these mutations. It only requires a small blood sample to determine the results. I was found to not have any mutation of these genes.

I faced my diagnosis of cancer by using the same coping methods I have used throughout my life. I grew up in an alcoholic family where I was not immune to physical, emotional, and sexual abuse. My method to survive and rise above this heritage was to use positive affirmations, a belief in God, and a burning desire to live free of that type of people and behavior. Then and now, I surround myself with family (some of whom I "adopted") and friends who can be powerful sources of strength and love.

I learned from my grandmother and adopted aunt that attitude, acceptance, and determination are important factors in healing the body, mind, and spirit. Those women were, and still are today, wonderful role models for me. They each succeeded in living healthy and productive lives through their positive attitudes, looking at life on earth as a stepping-stone to an even greater place. They worked hard and saw each obstacle as a challenge. Thanks to them, I have always used the word *challenge* instead of *problem*, *test*, or *trial*. I like *challenge* because I envision positivity, winning, learning, and growing.

I share my daily journey with ovarian cancer to educate, support, and inspire others. My journey is my own unique experience, though, and it's *not* intended to reflect what anyone else should expect as her experience. I encourage readers to share their own experiences and opinions on my website: **outshineovariancancer.com**. That said, I do believe some of the ways I have responded to and coped with this challenge may be of help to other women and their caregivers. We can all learn from one another, as well as support and help one another.

An important lesson I learned early in life is that the beauty of the soul, the real me and the real you, outshines the effects of cancer, chemotherapy, and radiation. It outshines any negative experience.

When things go wrong, as they sometimes will,
When the road you're trudging seems all uphill...
Stick to the fight when you're hardest hit,
It's when things seem worst that you mustn't quit.

—Joe O'Keefe

PHASE I

Detection

Chapter 1

D-day

The bright summer day started off full of activity, promise, and good thoughts. I was glad to get my annual mammogram and Pap (Papanicolaou) smear done in one day that particular Thursday. It meant I didn't have to make two trips to Edina, maneuvering the heavy construction and traffic. I got my mammogram done first, which went smoothly, despite some sore ribs under my breasts from a bad fall two weeks earlier.

As I waited in Dr. R's ob-gyn office, it seemed every woman was young or pregnant. As I watched them hold their large abdomens or tend to their newborns, it brought back happy memories of my own three pregnancies. I had always wanted a large family, like in the movie *Cheaper by the Dozen*, starring Clifton Webb and Jeanne Crain. I thought raising children would follow a perfect script, and we would all live happily ever after, erasing the memories of my abusive childhood. Instead of twelve kids, I had three sons, who are such wonderful gifts from God that I could never be happier being their mother. I did not mind all the testosterone that flowed through the house, and I never really minded not having a daughter.

Soon I found myself in the exam room, wearing the small tissue gown, sitting on the hard table, answering my doctor's questions, and feeling confident and proud of my good health. My confidence soon changed when Dr. R had difficulty inserting the speculum, causing me unusual discomfort. As she manually checked my abdomen and pelvis, she said, "I feel a mass." That's when I began to tremble. Trying to comfort me, she said, "It's probably a fibroid, but we need an ultrasound to make sure." A fibroid is a benign tumor found in or around the uterus. An ultrasound uses sound waves to see such body parts as organs, muscles, and tendons, as well as tumors.

I fought back the tears as I drove home, determined to put forth a strong and positive front to my husband, Jim. This is the second marriage for both of us, and in our twenty-four years together, we have truly grown to know each other very well. We came into the relationship each having three children. We truly consider our six kids and twelve grandchildren as "ours." Once I arrived home, he asked questions that I tried to answer succinctly, but he knows me too well, and he sensed the fear I was trying to hide. We have always shared everything and have had a mutual respect for each other, so there are no secrets or lies.

That night in bed, I let my hand slide down to the very lowest part of the left side of my abdomen, and I could feel a round lump. "Oh, God, I can feel it."

Jim palpated my abdomen and quietly said, "Yes, I can, too." We both started to cry as we tried to reassure each other, saying, "It's probably nothing."

☙

The following morning, Dr. R called to inform me that instead of an ultrasound, I would be having a CT (computed tomography) scan, which provides a cross-sectional view of internal body parts. I was instructed not to eat or drink anything prior to the test, which was scheduled for 1:00 in the afternoon. I told her I could now feel the lump in my lower left abdomen, so she asked me to see her in the office before having the scan. We quickly showered, dressed, and left the house to be in her

Edina office by 11:00 a.m. Just before opening our front door, we hugged and kissed.

Jim and I nervously waited for the doctor in the small exam room, and we kept looking at one another, sending love and reassurance. Dr. R again examined me, discussed the possible causes—from a fibroid to a cancerous tumor—and answered our questions as best she could. As she left the room, she promised to call with the CT results, even if they came in during the weekend.

That whole weekend was a like a nightmare I could not wake up from. The tears flowed almost without stopping. Sleeping and eating were almost impossible. Jim and I prayed and talked as we held each other tightly.

℘

So began my own personal D-day of June 6, except I was the one being invaded by some kind of a mass or tumor. On Sunday morning, we called the doctor, as the agony of not knowing the scan results was overwhelming. She apologized for not getting back to me sooner and then said, "I want to get an MRI right away Monday morning. The CT scan shows a mass that appears to be outside the uterus, which is not good. I cannot say for sure what the mass is, so that's why we need the MRI." Just before she hung up, she said, "I am so sorry, Karen."

Magnetic resonance imaging (MRI) uses radio waves, magnetism, and a computer. The MRI is a large, round machine that is impressive just by its size. On Monday morning, the technician called my name, instructed me on disrobing and removing any jewelry, showed me the gown and robe to put on, and then led me into a large room. She was very pleasant, kind, and soft-spoken, and she had a gentle spirit about her. I lay down on the slender table and immediately asked for a warming blanket, as the sterile-like coolness of the room surrounded me. The technician explained the process, the importance that I remain still during the test, and that there would be loud sounds like jackhammers. I smiled, nodded, allowed the blanket to warm me, closed my eyes, and began to meditate. I remained in a meditative state of abdominal breathing, focusing on God's healing light, and repeating words of comfort and peace.

Once the MRI was complete, the technician instructed me to get dressed and then sit in the main waiting room to be sure the films were okay for the radiologist to read. Then an unusual thing happened that left a deep impression on me. It is a lesson for those in the healthcare field to be mindful of what they say and how they say it. After about ten minutes, the same technician came up to me and said, "You may leave now. Your doctor will call you with the results." When I stood up to leave, she gave me a hug and whispered, "I'll pray for you."

I knew her heart was in the right place and her intentions were beautiful, but her words filled me with a terrible fear. I thought, I must surely be on death's doorstep with my body full of cancer. Did she hug every patient? Did she tell everyone she would pray for them?

The MRI confirmed the presence of a large mass outside the uterus. As a registered nurse, I knew there was a very good chance the tumor could be cancerous.

I have learned that any rain that falls in my life is just droplets, and it's up to me whether I will let those droplets flood away my spirit. Sometimes we need to build up levees through more prayer, erect dams for permanent changes so the soul can grow, do a dance to pray for more sun to heal any wounds, or just take an umbrella to give temporary protection as we build up our strength and will.

Open the eyes of my heart, O Lord, I want to see you.

—Ephesians 1:18

Chapter 2

Appointment with a Gynecological Oncologist

On Monday afternoon, Dr. R's office called to say they would arrange an appointment with the Minnesota Oncology group and needed to know if I preferred the Woodbury or Edina clinic locations. Since we lived equidistant from each city, I chose Edina. A short time later, I was informed that a Dr. Matthew Boente would see me the following day at 2:40 p.m.

At the same time I was on the telephone with Dr. Boente's office, Jim was at the jewelry shop of our good friend, Mort, to pick up his repaired wristwatch. Jim told him about my health situation, and Mort said, "There is only one doctor for Karen to see. I'll write his name down for you. He's the best gynecological oncology surgeon in the state of Minnesota. My niece did her residency under his tutelage." He wrote down the name. It was Matthew Boente!

Our son, Michael, came with Jim and me to meet Dr. Boente. I felt strongly that I wanted one of our kids there to hear what the doctor said and to also be there for Jim. Emotions can change our ability to hear things. In the waiting room, Jim and Michael talked about family, work, sports, and politics while I filled out three sheets of medical questionnaires before joining their conversation.

A young woman in her late twenties or early thirties was there with her husband and parents. She was also filling out papers, and I wondered what possible reason there could be for such a healthy looking young lady to be in an oncology clinic.

An hour later, she and her family were escorted down a hallway behind a closed door.

The three of us waited one and a half hours before we were finally called in at 4:30 p.m. The exam room was extremely small as we each managed to find a place to sit or stand. Suddenly the door opened, and a handsome, middle-aged gentleman walked in and introduced himself, "I'm Matt Boente." He shook each of our hands and looked us in the eyes, smiling and saying, "It's nice to meet you." My faith in Dr. Boente had been strong even before I met him, and after that first appointment, I knew God had put me in his care. Dr. Boente's specialty is surgery for cancer of the female organs.

Dr. Boente said he had talked to Dr. R and reviewed my MRI in more detail. "Tell me what you have been experiencing. Have there been any changes in your body that you are aware of?"

"Well," I said, "I have had an increase in my waist size, despite more exercising and diet changes. I have never had a weight problem, so this is all new to me." I paused and looked over at Jim before continuing on. "For the past week, I have had mucus around my stools, and they have been harder and smaller than usual." We had both been concerned about those symptoms and what they meant. I quickly added, "But I have always had constipation problems. My dad and sister have the same thing." I wanted to diminish my real concerns and fears that this was yet another sign of cancer.

Dr. Boente nodded. "Well, your MRI shows a mass the size of a honeydew melon, so that would certainly account for the changes in your waistline." Jim, Michael, and I were shocked to hear these words, looking at one another with wide eyes and dropped mouths. Dr. Boente held up his hands in a circle, bringing more reality to the size of the mass. I could not imagine anything that large in me, and all I could think was I wanted it out—right then and now.

Dr. Boente explained, "The tumor might be pushing on or has actually invaded your colon." He waited for each of us to absorb this new information. "Usually a mass this size is not malignant, but we will not know for sure until we operate and have pathology look at it. We will schedule you for a complete hysterectomy and tumor removal right away."

When he was about to leave the room, he apologized that we had to wait so long to be seen. After talking to Dr. R, he had squeezed me into his already busy schedule. He also explained that another woman was referred to him the same day, and he did not want to turn either of us away. "Some cases are quite advanced by the time I see them. Time is critical." His face showed sadness and frustration that ovarian cancer can be so aggressive.

Once he closed the door, we looked at each other, wondering if time was on my side. I prayed it was for me—and for the young lady who had been in the waiting room. As a nurse, I knew enough about ovarian cancer to realize it has a high fatality rate. But after five days of hearing and experiencing negative and frightening information, I was ready to hang on to a little hope. We were ready to see at least a glimmer of light shine through the darkness. The three of us had a nice supper, feeling more relaxed, informed, and ready to face the future.

No matter how good things are in your life, there is always something bad that needs to be worked on...
And no matter how bad things are in your life, there is always something good you can thank God for.
—Rick Warren

Chapter 3

Prayer and Love

It's said that as tears flow out, love flows in. I believe that to be true. For the next two weeks, a lot of love flowed in. Jim and I sobbed until our throats and stomachs ached. The week was painfully difficult while we waited for answers; informed our kids, family, and friends; and made preparations for surgery and recovery. It was the start of a journey that would have us enter hell and then travel various peaks and valleys of hope, fear, ministry, doubt, prayer, and an ever-closer relationship with God and each other.

I have always believed in God, even though I was raised in a home where there was no talk of God, Jesus, or the Bible. We never went to church, grace was only said when my stepfather's family was at our house for a meal, Easter was about the bunny rabbit, and Christmas was about Santa Claus. My grandmother, Edith, was the one who taught me about God, all religions, and how Jesus was her Savior.

In my junior year of high school, the abuse had escalated to a point where I knew my life was in danger. I left my mother's house in Long Beach, California, to live with my dad and his wife in Hollywood, California. Starting in my preteen years, my dad and I had become very close. He did not know about the abuse, because I was scared to tell him the "secret." The move meant changing schools, making new friends, and seeing very little of my mother and two sisters. Both sets of my grandparents had always been very important to me, and now they were even more so. Both Dad and my grandparents provided the stability, strength, and spiritual and religious beliefs I needed. It was an ending and a beginning, frightening and safe, confusing and sane, nightmare and dream, sadness and happiness. A classmate invited me to the youth group at her church every Wednesday night. So began my journey in truly knowing and accepting God into my life through Jesus the Christ. My faith has never stopped growing, and it was the foundation for which I found the strength and courage to face what lay ahead.

&

The time before my surgery gave Jim and me an opportunity to come to a new level of grief. We talked about the power of prayer and how our love could see us through anything. Prayer and love had already seen us through some difficult times with family, careers, and our own relationship.

We were overwhelmed, too, with the love and support we received from family and friends. Every message in a card, whether written by Hallmark or the sender, touched my heart and soul in a completely unexpected way. I learned a lesson in life that any birthday, sympathy, or get-well card might be very meaningful and powerful for the receiver. Therefore, cards need to be selected and sent with the ministry they are intended to have. Too many times in the past, I have sent cards without paying close attention to the words inscribed. *I gotta get this in the mail*, was my thought as I quickly selected a card after barely scanning the verse. That was not ministering to others. Rather, it was being too self-absorbed in my own busy-ness. Being on the receiving end of so many special cards opened my eyes and heart.

As the days brought us closer to the surgery, I learned that friends are one of the most cherished gifts I appreciate. One morning, I joined my dear friend, Charlotte, for a cup of coffee.

We had met twenty years ago when we worked together in the hospital's epilepsy unit. Sharing the same philosophy of life and nursing, we quickly formed a deep friendship. We talked about my upcoming surgery and the unknown challenges that lay ahead of me. She helped me deeply explore and discuss my true fears.

"I think my greatest fear is for Jim," I said. "How will he be if I die?" For over twenty years, we had lived each day as if we would live forever, though we had buried his parents and said goodbye to other relatives and friends. "Jim and I have such a close bond, it's like we're one. We're best friends, besides loving each other so deeply and profoundly."

Charlotte took my hand and said, "Jim is a survivor. He'll go through his stages of grief and will miss you terribly, but he'll survive just because of his love for you. He knows that's what you would want." After a few minutes she added, "Besides, none of us knows when we're going to die. Just because you might have cancer does not mean you are automatically going to die from it."

&

Knowing a long medical journey might lie ahead for me, I began to explore my options for complementary therapies I could use in conjunction with traditional medicine. My grandmother, Edith, believed in various health regimens such as herbs, Oriental medicine, homeopathy, and osteopathy. She also studied and practiced different forms of Christian and Eastern meditations. As I stated earlier, I was influenced by her healthy and balanced life.

Beginning in the early 1980s, I had been trained and educated in complementary therapies, so I knew about the different options I was researching. In 1986, I developed my own nursing service called Kare 'N Touch, where I offered counseling, massage, stress management, biofeedback, and energy work. As I faced my surgery, recovery, and possible cancer treatment, I was now turning to others for help, just as I had helped others. Everything took on a different meaning, as the information was for my own health.

I looked on the Internet for information on vitamin and mineral supplements, meditation, herbs, Reiki, Therapeutic Touch, and Healing Touch. One therapy that interested me is called Qigong, which is the basis of all Chinese medicine, dating back some four thousand years. It's based on the philosophy of bringing balance and harmony physically, mentally, and spiritually through meditation, breathing techniques, and movement. I remembered my grandmother talking about Qigong when she studied Asian religious and medical beliefs and practices.

A week before my surgery, I contacted Well Within in West St. Paul and received some Reiki energy healing. Reiki is a Japanese healing technique that works with the energy fields of the body. It provides deep relaxation and a sense of wellbeing. During that session, I became aware of my need to forgive myself in relationship to certain people. The teaching of forgiveness is a basic tenet of Christianity. It's not always an easy thing to do, but very necessary for a peaceful life, just as Jesus demonstrated so often.

I don't remember when, but at some point I had written down the following prayer by St. Francis of Assisi, which had now become powerfully comforting. The day before surgery, I printed a copy of it, carefully folded the paper in fourths, and taped the four sides. I would have it in my hands, holding it close to my heart, right up to the time they were ready to wheel me into surgery.

Lord, help me to live this day quietly, easily.
To lean upon thy great strength trustfully, restfully.
To wait for the unfolding of thy will patiently, serenely.
To meet others peacefully, joyously.
To face tomorrow confidently, courageously.

—St. Francis of Assisi

PHASE II

A New Life

Chapter 4

Surgery

This was the day I learned the truth about what was going on inside my body. My surgery was scheduled for 10:30 in the morning on June 20, exactly two weeks after the initial CT scan showed an abdominal mass. While I waited in pre-op, I found comfort by repeating the folded-up prayer by St. Francis of Assisi. When they were ready to wheel me into surgery, I handed the prayer to Jim, we kissed, and we said, "I love you." I closed my eyes, embracing the comforting words of the prayer, knowing Jim's love for me, and trusting God working through Dr. Boente.

Before surgery, I was told that a "simple" hysterectomy would take only two to three hours, but if there were cancer, it would be a five-to-six hour procedure. When I finally opened my eyes in recovery and saw the clock reading 4:30 p.m., I moaned, "Oh, no," and started to cry. With compassion in his eyes, Dr. Boente said, "I am so sorry."

That day, I went in and out of sleep, trying to assimilate this new challenge in my life.

> *Today, sad tears are in your eyes and mine,*
> *But look about for each bright ray of sunshine:*
> *Cherish them, for in the days ahead*
> *They will light your path.*
>
> —Dr. LaJune Foster

Chapter 5

Recovery and Healing

I was in the hospital a week for my surgical recovery, which proceeded without any complications. Each day, I slowly regained my physical and emotional strength, relying on my faith in God, a will to live, and support from family and friends. I also relied on my positive attitude to better cope and give my body the best environment to heal. It's well documented that the body will heal much more easily and quickly if a person maintains a positive attitude.

But still, for the first few days, I could not talk about cancer. I was in one of the early stages of grief—too much shock to fully absorb it. Gradually, though, I began to ask Dr. Boente questions, listened to him and the nursing staff, and talked with Jim and others. I learned how hard the wait had been for Jim and the family, since the surgery took five hours. As the hours passed, they knew it wasn't just a routine hysterectomy.

Dr. Boente reported that the mass, my left fallopian tube and ovary, and the outer layer of the lower section of my colon were cancerous, and so was the saline wash of my pelvic cavity. My particular type of cancer cell is called malignant mixed Mullerian tumor (MMMT), a sarcoma that's an aggressive and rare form of ovarian cancer. I was given a 50 percent chance of survival and graded at a Type IIC. The good news was that there was no cancer in the omentum (a large fold of fat that descends from the stomach and covers the intestines), the lymph glands that carry white blood cells and immune cells throughout the body, or my other organs. He did a complete hysterectomy, removing the ovaries, fallopian tubes, uterus, and cervix, as well as the omentum, several lymph glands, and eighteen inches of the lower bowel. Jim and the family tried to reassure me that Dr. Boente was confident he had successfully removed all the cancer, but those were empty words. I could only think about the word *cancer*. Unfortunately, a doctor can never be 100 percent sure all the cancerous tissue has been removed.

I came to understand that chemotherapy, my otherwise healthy body, my philosophy of life, and my personality were all important factors toward recovery. Dr. Boente said, "Karen, you're a very healthy sixty-seven-year-old woman with low blood pressure, a strong heart, healthy organs and bones, and normal weight. Your only problem is you have cancer! Many of my patients do not have these factors in their favor."

My friend, Charlotte, visited me in the hospital and spoke about the need to focus on the now. "Karen, do what's necessary to get strong and well enough to go home. I know you have all the spiritual, physical, and emotional capabilities to conquer this." As she left, she said, "I needed to see you with my own eyes. Now I know you'll be okay. You look really good."

❧

Jim came to the hospital every morning and stayed until suppertime. With each passing day, I could see he was becoming more tired.

"Honey, you don't have to stay here all day," I said. "I'm in good hands." Yet there he was, bright and early every morning, bringing the newspaper, cards, and telephone messages. He helped me untangle the IV tubing, walk to the bathroom, sit in the chair, or take several walks in the hall.

One evening around 7:30 p.m., he was fighting to keep his beautiful blue eyes open. Since I, too, was feeling exceptionally tired, he reluctantly agreed to go home. An hour later, just as I received my evening medications and found a comfortable position, I sensed someone was in the room. I opened my eyes, turned toward the shadow in the light from the hallway, and saw a figure quietly standing there.

"May I help you?" I asked. I thought a visitor had entered the wrong room.

"Karen, it is Robyn. Jim wanted me to come over and stay with you." I recognized my daughter-in-law's voice. "Jim called because he thinks you need someone here with you."

I reassured her I was okay and that she could go home to her family. I appreciated Jim's concern, but at that moment, all I wanted was to sleep. I did not want or need anyone with me.

Robyn sat down, lifted her book to the hallway light, and said, "I'll just sit here and read until you fall asleep."

This event demonstrated two things: One, it showed the role of family to help one another without any conditions or rewards. You help just because you love and care about the person. But two, it was a lesson distinguishing *caretaking* from *caregiving*. For example, we *take care* of children or adults unable to make decisions for themselves. We *give care* to capable individuals who request care when they are in need—and the type of care we each request is unique to us. Some people literally want someone to hold their hand, while others do not like to be touched at all.

The next morning, Jim and I talked about these two aspects of caring. I thanked him for his thoughtfulness and desire to help me, but I said, "I'm not you. When I don't feel well, I like to be left alone. I pray, think, or sleep. On the other hand, you like to have someone with you all the time. A perfect example is when you were in the hospital for a week after your colon resection. You wanted me there from early morning to late in the evening. One time you had your son stay with you all night."

Jim listened and nodded in agreement. "I'm sorry. I felt guilty that I left you last night. That's why I called Robyn. I didn't want you to be alone in the hospital." He paused and then said, "I guess I was taking care of you instead of giving care."

I smiled and said, "I love you for loving me so much. I know your intentions were beautiful and you thought you were doing what was best for me." He reached down to me in the bed, and then we hugged and kissed with tears of love in our eyes.

Happy moments, PRAISE GOD
Difficult moments, SEEK GOD
Quiet moments, WORSHIP GOD
Painful moments, TRUST GOD
Every moment, THANK GOD

—Rick Warren

Chapter 6

Ministering Touch

I believe in the power of loving and healthy touch, and I held tight to that belief during my hospital stay. The thesis for my master's degree was titled, "Loving Touch: One Step to Health." It discussed in detail how the whole body's physiology responds in a positive way to loving touch. Such responses include endorphin release, muscle relaxation, increased blood flow, decreased nerve stimulation, and slowed heart and respiratory rates. Skin is our largest sense organ, and all too often, many of us are hesitant to touch another, even a loved one. A gentle touch on the hand or shoulder can relieve tension, and for some people, a hug will calm fears and help them feel accepted and loved. As a nurse and massage therapist, I have often witnessed the benefit of such touch. Some massage clients were able to release painful memories from abusive touch and learned to accept touch that was kind and comforting.

While in the hospital, I was very aware of how often the nurses placed a hand on my shoulder, arm, or hand with complete ease while they answered questions, assessed my pain, or offered suggestions. The staff responded to my request for any complementary care that might be available. A registered nurse who was head of the alternative care department did some Therapeutic Touch, which works with energy fields to promote healing. It's a discipline that has gained recognition and acceptance by the medical and scientific worlds. I was receiving help in the very area I once offered to so many people through my nursing service, Kare 'N Touch. The experience was peaceful and left me with a sense of power over my body and emotions. It connected me even more deeply to my spiritual side.

The day I was discharged, two of the nurses gave me a hug and encouraged me to call if I had any questions or concerns once I was home. As difficult and painful my reason was for being at Southdale Hospital, I experienced such excellent care. It made this part of my journey easier than what it might have been otherwise. I thank each of the staff members for all their kindness, expertise, and spirit.

It's not where you end up,
It's the journey you take.
—Anonymous

Chapter 7

Finding Emotional and Physical Strength

While I was in the hospital, I asked a nurse for a piece of paper so I could write thoughts or questions as they arose. She brought me a wonderful purple five-by-seven spiral-bound notebook. It was so very helpful and useful to journal in it during my hospitalization. I still use it to this day for my appointments with oncologists, or just to write down thoughts related to my cancer.

Sometime when I was in elementary school, I started writing in a diary, sometimes every day. I can still see the little book with its strap that locked all my secrets in its pages. Other diaries, notebooks, and journals followed. I have always found it helpful to write my thoughts, questions, dreams, or fears. In the last thirty years, I have written poems, short stories, or pieces of prose in addition to writing in diaries. Whatever form it takes, journaling is an excellent way for me to find clarity.

At my first clinic appointment two weeks after my discharge, I asked Dr. Boente several questions from that purple notebook. He took the time to answer all the questions to both Jim's and my satisfaction. The more information we had, the better we were able to cope and make decisions.

One question was about the CA125 blood test. He explained that the CA125 test measures a protein that may be elevated in women with ovarian cancer. It's not 100 percent reliable, as the protein can also be elevated in such conditions as endometriosis (when cells from within the uterus appear outside the uterus), other benign diseases, and even pregnancy. Also, not every patient with cancer has high CA125 test results. At the time of my surgery, my CA125 was 79; the normal range is 0 to 35.

Looking back at my notebook, I next asked, "When you said the MMMT was aggressive, does that mean my cancer is incurable?"

Dr. Boente explained that there are three common subtypes of ovarian cancer tumors—epithelial, germ cell, and stromal—whereas an MMMT like mine is a rare form. Not only is it rare, but it is also quite aggressive. However, Dr. Boente said it does respond well to chemotherapy.

Dr. Boente palpated my abdomen and examined my incision. He asked questions about my bowels, urination, appetite, and level of energy. He instructed me to continue eating five small meals a day and to take multivitamins, Boost or Ensure, and L-Glutamine. L-Glutamine is the most abundant amino acid found in blood plasma. It is an important part of healing and regenerating the body.

"You can do any exercise in moderation," Dr. Boente also said, "but do avoid lifting anything heavier than two pounds for now. Taking daily walks one to two times a day is a wonderful way to strengthen the body and increase stamina. In time, you can increase your activities."

I was pleased with his answer. I have done yoga and some form of exercise for most of my life. If I was not exercising, I was dancing. As a child, I took ballet, tap dance, and gymnastics. In high school and college, I was in water ballet, volleyball, and yoga.

"You're doing well," he said. "Keep up the good work. You will still need chemotherapy, which we'll start in two weeks." I would get Taxol and carboplatin, the two most commonly used drugs for ovarian cancer, every three weeks for a total of six infusions.

Upon arriving home I went right to my computer, where I researched ovarian cancer, MMMT, and the chemotherapy drugs carboplatin and Taxol. To read blogs and articles about my particular cancer cell was often depressing, negative, and discouraging. I found myself focusing on the negativity of cancer, and I began to allow fear to control my life. It was helpful to be informed about the drugs and their potential side effects, but I had to redirect my thinking to healing and health, so whatever time I had left on this earth could be productive and happy.

I gradually regained my strength every day by increasing my activities. Each morning, I got up, dressed, and made the bed. I tried to do some kind of housework so I felt like I was still a contributing member of the household. With Jim by my side, I first walked half a block, then a whole block, and eventually achieved one mile twice a day. I supplemented my meals with a bottle of Ensure, just as I had encouraged my ninety-five-year-old dad to do for the past few years.

During my rest periods, I watched old episodes of *I Love Lucy*, *Leave It to Beaver*, *The Carol Burnett Show*, or any movie or show that would make me laugh. Research by Norman Cousins in the 1980s showed the positive and healing effects of laughter on the biochemistry of our bodies. I personally believe he was correct in his theory. Besides, it was more fun to laugh than to cry or be depressed.

I continued to receive such loving ministry from my friends and family, to which I attribute so much to my recovery. One such person who ministered to me was a lady I call Aunt Arleigh. I adopted her as my aunt when I was sixteen years old. She became a very important and influential person in my life. She was so full of life, always positive, and had a smile that would warm any heart. She was only sixteen years older than me, yet she taught me so many things about life. The night of my high school prom, she helped me dress, fix my hair, and put on some makeup. It was Aunt Arleigh who greeted my date, helped pin my corsage, and was waiting for me when I came home. That is just one example of the kind of person she is to this day. God bless her!

Aunt Arleigh put me in contact with Silent Unity, a group of people who pray 24/7 and whose prayer chain has not been broken in 180 years. She also suggested I try "channeling down," which is a method of prayer used by the Quakers. It helped me hear God, rather than me just tell Him what I wanted. She lovingly instructed me to stop saying, "I *have* cancer," but instead say, "I *had* cancer." She was reinforcing the teaching of positive thinking, which was popularized by Norman Vincent Peale in the 1950s.

Jim and I did better each day as we adjusted to this new phase of our lives. We woke up each morning with a smile, rejoicing we had another day to enjoy each other. One or both of us would occasionally have a weak time and need to cry, but from each experience, we had wonderful talks and came out of it stronger than before.

> *We cannot direct the wind,*
> *But we can adjust our sails.*
> —Bertha Calloway

Tests and Treatments

Chapter 8

Facing Reality

I was scheduled for a PET (positron emission tomography) scan a few days before my first chemotherapy. This type of scan measures such things as blood flow, oxygen use, and glucose metabolism to help identify any abnormal functioning of organs. It was my first time to have this test, though as a nurse, I had scheduled it for many patients in the hospital where I worked.

In preparation for the PET scan, I drank some glucose, and then a radioactive tracer was intravenously injected into my arm. None of this was painful or uncomfortable, and the technician was very kind and helpful. After about a half hour, I was escorted into the scan room, where the large machine with its very narrow table greeted me. The room was cool, so the technicians quickly covered me with warm blankets before they strapped me onto the table. "You will need to remain very still and lay your arms flat on the table above your head," one of the technicians instructed.

As I had done for MRI and CT scans, I closed my eyes and began meditating, asking the Christ Spirit to be with me. I did deep abdominal breathing, imagined rays of white light flowing through me, and repeated words and phrases of love and healing. I was only aware of my environment and the increasing discomfort in my arms when the technician interrupted my meditation with words of explanation or encouragement.

After the PET scan, Jim and I attended a chemotherapy class with one other couple. The word *chemotherapy* creates fear in most people. We often think of pain, baldness, vomiting and diarrhea, and, possibly, eminent death. Chemotherapy was first introduced in the 1930s. During World War I and II, scientists found that people who died after exposure to mustard gas had weakened or destroyed bone marrow and lymph nodes. That was the beginning for treating lymphoma, cancer of the lymph glands. Chemotherapy has come a long way in prolonging life or curing cancer. The medical field has also been able to lessen or eliminate its side effects. Chemo can slow cancer's growth, kill cancer cells, and keep them from spreading. Unfortunately, it cannot differentiate between a healthy cell and a cancer cell.

During the class, we learned more about the chemo treatment and its side effects. I knew from my Internet research that one of the side effects of Taxol and carboplatin is hair loss. Yet, to hear someone say those words out loud, directed at me and another lady, was quite a difficult experience. We both cried while our husbands tried to comfort us. "Your hair will grow back," the nurse assured me. But at that moment, her words were not comforting or reassuring. I only vaguely heard her discuss other possible side effects. Fortunately, she gave handouts to each of us. From the time Dr. R first discovered the mass and I had the CT and MRI tests, my emotions had been preventing me from retaining and understanding information. Journaling and having Jim's help were so valuable in helping me process everything.

The nurse escorted us on a tour of the large chemotherapy room, which was divided into three sections, each with La-Z-Boy chairs and flat-screen TVs. Fortunately, there were earphones for each television. The nurse's station was situated so all the chairs were in clear view. High windows overlooking a busy, tree-lined avenue provided lots of natural light. Women and men all directly touched by cancer sat in the large, comfortable chairs with intravenous poles, bags, and tubes next to them. For most of them, a spouse, family member, friend, or caregiver sat nearby, offering support through conversation, food, or assistance.

As the tour came to an end, I realized so much had happened in just three weeks, at times life seemed surreal. Jim helped keep my feet firmly planted on the ground, and I clung to my faith that everything was in God's hands.

I know that God in Heaven holds each hand,
Even as He helps me to understand.

—Dr. LaJune Foster

Chapter 9

Trials of Chemo

Three weeks after my surgery, I walked into the clinic for the start of my first chemotherapy treatment. The waiting room was full, and we had to wait an hour for my treatment to begin. I quietly and prayerfully observed the other men and women there. I tried to glean information from their behavior, demeanor, and conversations. I saw some who looked quite pale and frail, while others were robust and energetic. Some people quietly read or, like me, watched people. I wondered how I would be after this new experience of chemotherapy. I prayed for courage and strength.

Then I heard my name, "Karen I.," called out. Jim and I were escorted through the door and into the chemo room. I soon found myself sitting in a La-Z-Boy. My nurse, Niels, was kind, efficient, and attentive. He explained each step of the process, which I found very helpful. I looked up at Jim while Niels hung the first IV bag. Our eyes shared our fears of the unknown and yet also our complete trust in Dr. Boente and the medical team. It was a strange mixture of feelings.

The whole process took about four and a half hours, and I slept for about one hour of it. Unfortunately, Jim had to sit on a hard, small chair across from me the whole time. We had packed a lunch, some books, and a deck of cards, but we both found it difficult to concentrate on anything. At one point, all the chairs in the treatment center were filled with people getting IVs for one kind of medicine or another. Most of them appeared to be fifty-five years or older, though one lady looked to be in her forties. Some had lost their hair, some looked very sick, and others looked perfectly healthy.

Despite the sadness of why each of us was in this room, there was a sense of peace, hope, and even laughter at times. I watched the nurses as they efficiently and professionally interacted with each patient, always wearing smiles with gentleness and kindness in their eyes. I knew I was in good hands.

We came home exhausted from our long, emotional, and physically tiring day. We let ourselves melt into the sheets of our bed, embraced in each other's arms, and took a nap. We had a quiet evening and a light dinner before calling our kids and sending out emails.

☙

The fourth day after chemotherapy, I felt very low in energy, constipated, and bored. I missed being more active and involved in life. Intellectually, I knew all the symptoms would improve, but it was hard to believe it then. I called the nurse, Ann, who reassured me that what I was experiencing was typical and would pass. She was soft spoken and kind, and she considered all my questions important.

Then two days later, I felt very good and rejuvenated, so we went to the zoo. It was my first big outing. It was good to be out among people who were well and enjoying their day. We had a wonderful lunch afterward, and though I was tired by the time we got home, it was from activity—not illness, surgery, or chemotherapy.

In the mail, I received two very special cards. The first one was from someone in Florida I considered a friend, but did not know very well. She wrote a personal note of support and good wishes and included a book of prayers for all occasions. Her thoughtfulness and kindness touched me deeply. Another friend sent a card with this piece of prose in it:

WHAT CANCER CANNOT DO

IT CANNOT...

INVADE THE SOUL

SUPPRESS MEMORIES

KILL FRIENDSHIP

DESTROY PEACE

CONQUER THE SPIRIT

SHATTER HOPE

CRIPPLE LOVE

CORRODE FAITH

STEAL ETERNAL LIFE

SILENCE COURAGE

—Author unknown

Chapter 10

Two Angels

I believe that people come into our lives for a definite purpose, and that is to learn and grow. Sometimes they are negative, evil, or bad people, but we are still to learn from them. I can use my childhood experiences with my stepfather as an example. I learned why abuse occurs and that it was not my fault. Once I forgave him, I was able to help other people who suffered from abuse. Fortunately, I have been blessed with many kind and beautiful souls who have taught me so much about me and my life. Two such people who deeply touched me are Janice and Athena.

When I was getting that first PET scan, Jim struck up a conversation with a young woman named Janice. She was sitting in the waiting room with her bald head uncovered. He told her he thought showing her bald head was beautiful. It turned out she was diagnosed with a very rare cancer that affected her whole body. She told Jim that when she first started losing her hair, she bought a wig. She brought it home and left it on the counter, where her nine-year-old son found it. He put it on, grabbed a broom, and began to pretend he was a rock singer playing the guitar. She realized then that her son did not care if she were bald, so why should she? She never wore it, and she put on a hat or scarf only when the Minnesota temperatures were too cold.

Jim shared with her about my struggle with the fact that I would lose my hair. She gave him her business card and said, "Tell your wife to call me. I would be glad to talk to her." The Lord does work in beautiful ways, and an angel had come into our lives.

I, too, was blessed to meet her the day of my first chemotherapy treatment. She introduced herself to me as she immediately recognized Jim from just a few days prior. We had a wonderful talk. She had such a positive attitude, it could help even the most cynical or fearful person. It turned out that Janice lived only a few miles from us in St. Paul. The story of how she became Dr. Boente's patient is one of God's miracles at work. She had been in a St. Paul hospital for what her oncologist determined was her last-chance treatment. Dr. Boente was the attending physician that weekend, and Janice's oncologist shared his frustration about her particular case and how he had no other options to offer her. Dr. Boente shared how he happened to have done a lot of research on her particular cancer. Janice readily accepted to go under his care.

"Your hair is not you," she told me. "*You* are you. Yes, people will look at you, but that's okay." As she left for her chemo treatment, she waved and signaled with her right hand, "Call me."

❧

The blessings just kept coming. One night, I received the most beautiful phone call from a dear friend, Athena, who had read my latest email regarding my impending hair loss. She shared that she has alopecia, which is a skin disease of the autoimmune system. It has left her completely bald, including her eyebrows and eyelashes. At the time we talked, she had been wearing a wig for fourteen years. I had no idea about the wig or the illness, though I had noticed she penciled her eyebrows. I had tears of admiration and respect as she told me her story of coping with the baldness, her relationships with men, and being seen in public without her wig. She also said she would be glad to go shopping with me for a wig, scarves, or hats, since she knew a place with a good selection. I eagerly accepted her offer and thanked her for the loving gift of sharing.

❧

These two angels helped me take a step toward accepting and coping with the eventual baldness. I decided to begin by cutting my shoulder-length hair very short. As she cut my hair, my hairdresser, Denise, said, "I'll come to your house and shave your head when you're ready. It'll be easier for you, Karen, if we do it in your own home. I've done this for a number of my clients and would be glad to do it for you."

My hair now was about as short as Jim's hair. He said, "You look like Jamie Lee Curtis—only more beautiful." What a wonderful thing to say.

> *Angels exist, but sometimes, since they don't*
> *all have wings,*
> *We call them FRIENDS.*
> —Author unknown

Chapter 11

Prayer and Faith

One night after getting my hair cut and the first round of chemo, I let fear and doubt take over my thinking. I tried to meditate, but the negative thoughts kept winning until I finally turned on the television and took a sleeping pill.

The next morning, Jim and I had a wonderful discussion about our level of activity and my occasional times of depression. At times, it was hard to have the mental and physical energy to do the things I loved to do. We agreed it was important to remember how far I had come, but also to start doing things for fun—going to the zoo, hitting golf balls, shopping, going to a movie, gardening. So we walked a mile, and then I pruned a small hedge. Both activities were excellent forms of therapy.

Later that afternoon, Dr. Boente's nurse, Ann, called. "Karen, the results of your PET scan were normal." This was the first scan since surgery.

I wanted to make sure I understood her correctly. "The scan showed *all* my vital organs and tissue?"

"Yes, and they're all clean. No cancer cells are showing," she repeated.

I started to cry tears of relief, thankfulness, and joy. It was very hard waiting for Jim to return home from his errands so I could tell him. Finally, he drove up, and I ran into his arms, saying, "There is no cancer." At first, he could not believe his ears, so I kept repeating, "There is no cancer." He, too, cried tears of joy and relief.

☙

Two days later, I went to my first Qigong class, which was wonderful and very healing. The meditative exercises could also be done on my own to help bring balance and healing. The small group of people was very friendly, and we introduced ourselves on a first-name basis only. The purpose of the group was to provide support through silent prayers for each other. Qigong invites each individual to choose his or her own spiritual guide. For me, that's Jesus the Christ. Then through gentle body postures and movements, each person meditates to bring healing to the group as well as themselves.

I have a wonderful picture of Jesus holding a lamb that I received from a former client, Kori. Several years ago, her husband was suddenly killed by a drunken driver while they were walking hand in hand down a sidewalk overlooking the Mississippi River. I had always loved this particular picture of Jesus, which I could look at in her home as I counseled and ministered to her. A few months after her husband's death, Kori gave me this picture, and it now hangs in the room where I used to see clients for Kare 'N Touch. I focused on this picture while I practiced Qigong several times a day. Often it was just an awareness of my breathing and the images of God's healing energy entering with each inhalation. I did at least one deep meditation a day, and each night I fell asleep doing another meditation. This helped me to the degree that most nights, I did not need to take any Ambien, a sleeping pill.

My cousin Farley, who has survived cancer, sent me a card with the following inspirational message about fear. The powerful words touched me deeply. Fear can be so debilitating. I used to counsel clients that our fears are usually greater than the reality of the situation, and that using prayer and imagery can often take away the power of fear. Now it was time for me to practice what I had taught others.

The Litany Against Fear

I must not fear
Fear is the mind killer
Fear is little-death that brings total obliteration
I will face my fear
I will permit it to pass over me and through me
And when it has gone past I will turn the inner eye
   to see its path
Where the fear has gone there will be nothing
Only I will remain.

—Frank Herbert

Chapter 12

Time to Make Plans

While I was recovering from surgery in the hospital, Dr. Boente said that, statistically, women in Stage IIC have a 50 percent survival rate of five years. He went on to say that the good news was that we had caught the cancer before it had advanced too far. However, the bad news was that the cancer cell was a sarcoma. That's all I remembered, because the outlook was not as encouraging as I had hoped.

After going through the stress of the surgery and the first of six rounds of chemotherapy, Jim and I were ready to discuss our thoughts about what we each wanted for a funeral and burial. Though the Grim Reaper seemed to be more at my doorstep, we both knew death could come to either of us at any time. Planning for a final resting place may seem morbid to some people, but for Jim and me, the reality of mortality had been set that June. We wanted to make clear, well-planned decisions for our sakes and for the kids'.

It's unfortunate that in our society death is not talked about until it happens to a loved one. It's interesting how we plan in great detail our weddings, the birth of children, birthdays, and anniversaries—yet not our funerals or wakes. Few people have any prearrangements regarding a funeral, memorial service, or cemetery. The same is true for living wills or estate wills. Instead, we depend on loved ones to make these decisions during very emotional times, and quite often, our loved ones are not always aware of what our wishes might be.

I watched my grandparents' coffins slide into crypts, visited my uncle's buried remains from World War II at Fort Rosecrans, and helped spread my mother's ashes into the Pacific Ocean. Me, I had always wanted to be cremated, because it seems more natural to give my remains back to the earth for trees, grasses, or flowers to grow. For years, I had instructed Jim and my sons to bury my ashes in the garden I had designed, tended, and loved at our St. Paul house. Now I realized the impracticality of such an act, because it was unrealistic that any member of my family would be able to visit my burial site. I could not visualize any of them knocking on the door years later and saying to the new homeowner, "My loved one's ashes are buried in your backyard. Would you mind if I pay my respects?"

Jim and I also agreed we wanted our ashes to be together. We began to share different ideas of how we might accomplish the wish to be together, be in the soil, and yet have a place for our family and friends to visit. Soon we were sharing our love for Lakewood Cemetery. It is so beautiful and easily accessible, and it has a very spiritual and peaceful chapel. Lakewood Cemetery is located in the heart of Minneapolis, only two blocks from where Jim lived as a child. In this quiet neighborhood, Jim had his paper route, rode his bicycle, and played catch. Every Sunday, his family walked to the nearby Church of the Incarnation for Mass. His father took him and his siblings to this same cemetery to learn how to drive. And now, both his parents are buried there.

We drove to the cemetery the next day and picked out a plot for our remains, finding the perfect spot surrounded by crabapple trees and looking toward a lake. We had hoped our ashes could be scattered right into the earth, but that is not allowed at this particular cemetery. Because we had often visited his parents' grave, we decided we would also have a marked grave. For one of our kids in particular, it's important that we have a marked site where she can visit those who have passed on. We agreed to have our remains together in one container that will hang suspended in a thirty-six-inch square block of granite.

Jim and I had beautiful discussions and cries about our deep and abiding love for each other. He shared his fear of the emptiness of life without me, and I replied about my fear of not being here with him. We were able to reach the point of knowing we had the gift to grieve together. How many of us are able or willing to talk to our loved ones about our own eminent death? Our children were also able to do some grieving with us, as they expressed their concerns and fears for the future. I thought of a dear friend, Judy, who died from a lung condition just within a year or two of her diagnosis. She and her husband, John, were able to grieve together and make arrangements, and she said goodbye to family and friends.

But sometimes death can come at any moment—sometimes without any warning or preparation. Time for grieving is not available to couples when one person dies suddenly and unexpectedly. A longtime friend, Jan, went downstairs in the middle of the night to find her husband had died in his sleep, lying on the couch in the living room. He had not been feeling well for a few days, but they assumed it was just a virus. Even a visit to the doctor did not reveal anything of concern.

As I thought about Jan, I allowed the fear of what Jim would do if I died first. How would he live his daily life? What would he do with my books, papers, sewing projects, writing, and so on? Would he sell both our homes, keep one, or keep both? There were so many questions. Yet who was I to suppose that I would be the first to die? Who was I to try to take care of Jim, when he is strong and responsible? As I recalled the following piece of prose, I was able to let go of my fears.

In the beginning—when God scattered stars into space—He planned treasures for us to discover—like love and life—and people like you.

—Flavia

Chapter 13

New Me

A few days after our trip to Lakewood Cemetery, two important events reshaped my role as a daughter and as a woman with cancer.

When the telephone's loud ring awoke us at 3:00 in the morning on August 1, I knew it had to be bad news. From Florida, the hospice nurse informed me that Dad had died. He had been in hospice care at an assisted living facility. Jim and I live in Florida six months out of the year, and when we left in May to return to Minnesota, his doctor and I had agreed hospice was appropriate with Dad's declining health.

On his birthday the previous April, he told me, "I have lived to see my ninety-fifth birthday, and now I am ready to go." He had celebrated his birthday with both his daughters, although the day was ominously filled with more tears than smiles. I believe we all sensed this would be his last. And I remember so clearly my last visit with him in May before we returned to Minnesota. He seemed so frail and small, sitting in his recliner, as we said good-bye. A part of me knew it would be the last time to see him alive, and yet I tried quickly to erase that thought. "We'll come down this summer and spend time with you," I said as I hugged him.

When I learned of my cancer in June, my telephone call to him from the hospital was difficult. How do you tell your parent his child has cancer? I tried to be optimistic and honest with him. He responded the best he ever knew how to respond to bad news: "Oh. I'm sorry to hear that." I knew what was in his heart, and yet he was unable to give any more support or encouragement than that.

Because of the timing of my chemotherapy, I wasn't able to be by his side as he made his final journey. Every day I talked to him on the phone and promised I would be there as soon as the doctor gave me permission to travel. I kept my promise, but unfortunately, Dad had already passed on. Jim and I visited his gravesite two weeks after his death. He had not wanted a funeral or memorial service, but I had prearranged his burial at the cemetery of his choosing. Now I was no longer a daughter, but the matriarch of the family. This was a role I had never anticipated.

⁊⁊

The second event took place the afternoon of Dad's death. We had previously arranged to meet Athena, our friend who has alopecia, at a store called Fantasia. There I sat in a chair, trying on hats, scarves, and wigs in preparation for the time when I would need them to cover my bald head. Athena and Jim gave their input about what looked good or not. We shared some good laughs and a few tears. I came home with four hats and a wig that matched my present salt-and-pepper haircut. I bought bottles of Nioxin shampoo and conditioner to use later on my bald head plus some Nioxin follicle booster to help slow down my eyebrow loss.

I couldn't fully visualize how I would look or react once I would lose all my hair, but the hats, scarves, and wig gave me a sense of security. I thought only about a bald head and did not think about total body baldness. It would be another month before I had to confront my loss of eyelashes, eyebrows, and pubic, arm, and leg hair.

❧

There in the store that afternoon, I looked in the mirror and saw myself in a different light. I'm sure Dad's death opened my eyes in a way they had not been opened before. I felt a mixture of sadness that Dad would not be there to help me, as he had helped me when I was that high school girl needing to be saved. Yet, I was glad he would not be here if I were to die in the near future.

Dad taught me to be strong and resourceful. Now I needed to embrace those qualities not as a cancer *victim*, but as a *survivor*. I prayed for strength and wisdom while I faced cancer and all that came with it. That day, I went a long way on my journey of acceptance toward my soon-to-be baldness. It was not easy, and I knew it was all due to my vanity, which was a life lesson. I was not as strong as Athena or Janice, the woman we met at the chemo center, but they were role models and inspirations to me. I wanted someday to be bald and proud of it.

There's an answer to the suffering you see, and though it isn't easy, it's still as simple as you and me.

—Author unknown

Chapter 14
Time to Journal, Time to Laugh

It had been three weeks since my first chemotherapy, and I approached my second round with a sense of familiarity. The thought of harsh medicines traveling through my body was still scary, but I didn't want to think of them as *poison* killing my healthy cells. During the infusion of the drugs, I instead used imagery to see the chemo molecules like knights in shining armor, slaying all the cancer cells.

I had some cramping and frequent bowel movements the day of the infusion, but otherwise everything went fine. The next day, I felt great and had lots of energy. The nurse called to report that my CA125 was 9.1. Such wonderful news, as it had been 74 before surgery and down to 39 before my first chemotherapy.

During the weeks after chemo, I concentrated on giving my white and red blood cells everything they needed to keep me alive through diet, exercise, supplements, meditation, and imagery. I filled each day with daily walks; journaling; tracking my intake of vitamins, minerals, and laxatives; doing Qigong for an hour or more; and keeping in contact with family and friends. Every day, I kept a written record of my bowel habits, physical symptoms, sleep patterns, and energy levels. Otherwise, I forgot or got confused about whether I had taken my various pills for nausea, elimination, general strengthening, sleep, or pain. Again, my little purple notebook was my method of journaling such information.

Despite my very short hair, I was like a cat shedding its fur in the spring. What little hair I had left was coming out in clumps when I shampooed. Hair was on my pillow every morning, and hair would fly in the air if I touched my head. One morning, Jim was brushing his teeth with our electric toothbrush (which is the only way to brush) when he felt something between his teeth. He couldn't tell exactly what it was, but as he flossed, out came one of my hairs! He began to laugh and immediately told me what happened. Once we both stopped laughing and wiped away our tears, I picked up the phone and called my hairdresser and friend, Denise. It was time to shave my head, and I was actually ready for it.

Two days later, I watched in my bathroom mirror as my hair fell away to reveal a bald head. It went better than I thought, since I had been preparing myself for so many weeks. While Denise shaved my head, we laughed and talked about kids, life, and shapes of heads. "You're one of the lucky ones, Karen. Your head is beautifully shaped," she said while she rubbed my shiny head with some lotion.

I showed her the Nioxin hair products, and she agreed they would be very good for my scalp. "Wash your head every day, and keep it protected from the sun," were her words of advice.

Jim kissed the top of my head and told me how much he loved me. I asked him to take pictures of me with a scarf, a hat, and then just my bald head, which we then sent to friends and family via email. This was a very big step in the healing process.

There would be many times when it would be hard to let my bald head show even in front of Jim, though I knew he loved me unconditionally and saw my beauty way beyond the physical. I needed to see my beauty in the same way. My friend, Athena, said, "One day, I was able to look in the bathroom mirror and truly see the essence of who I really am." That was so beautiful. God bless her.

If you focus on your problems, you're going into self-centeredness. . . .
Get your focus off yourself and onto God and others.

—Rick Warren

Chapter 15

Comforting Outreach

I saw the nurse practitioner, Jackie, instead of Dr. Boente just prior to my third chemotherapy treatment. We decided Dr. Boente must have felt encouraged about my progress, since he scheduled me with his nurse instead of himself. My CA125 was down to 7.5, which again brought great relief and a sense of hope to both Jim and me.

From my little purple notebook, I asked Jackie questions. We discussed my impending eyebrow and eyelash loss, which I was truly dreading. Though my heart sank, I thought of Athena, and I asked God to help me be more like her. Jackie also reviewed the significance of aggressive MMMT, but finished by saying, "I have seen many women do very well for several years with your type of cancer." I knew she could not be more specific, but still, I wanted her to tell me, "You will be cured."

Going through this health challenge was certainly not something I would wish on anyone, but some beautiful things came as a result of it. So many people helped me gain confidence and strength to get through the tough times. Their words, prayers, and acts of kindness through visits, gifts, or phone calls touched my soul. From a friend in Florida, I received three knitted hats to wear during our cooler Minnesota days. The colors were pink, light green, and yellow. According to one of my knitting books, *The Prayer Shawl Ministry*, each color has meaning. For pink, it's joy, friendship, and femininity; for green, it's healing, harmony, and safety; and for yellow, it's cheerfulness, energy, and confidence. In the past, I had used this book to make shawls and scarves for hospice, the sick, and shut-ins. Now it was my turn to receive.

Another Florida friend sent me a stuffed animal her sister had hugged and held during a serious illness a few years prior. There were times when I buried my face in its soft body and let it absorb my tears. Someday I will pass this comforting and cute animal on to others in need. God was at work to help me see people in the Light.

&

My younger sister, Denise, and her husband, Randy, visited from Vancouver, Washington, three months after my diagnosis. It was very therapeutic for me to spend time with them as we laughed, shared, and prayed together. We hugged, cried, talked, played games, then cried and laughed some more. They rubbed my bald head and said, "You're beautiful."

The four of us went to our son Michael's house for his daughter Gabrielle's eighth birthday party, filling the house with more laughter and talks. My son immediately wanted to see my bald head that he rubbed and said, "Mom, it looks great." I gave Gabby a quilt her great-great-grandmother had made for me when I was Gabby's age. I included a picture of my grandmother and wrote about her journey in life. It was a rite of passage of a woman's role in the family. It was also the right time to pass on a keepsake from one generation to the next.

One morning, Denise and I went to my favorite coffee shop, Brewberry's, for a cup of white chocolate mocha. Of course, we got the largest size and sat for over an hour, just talking girl stuff. We talked about our kids and our own childhood, but mostly we talked about me and my cancer. It's one thing to talk about the loss of a grandparent or parent, but it's unusual and painful to contemplate the death of a sibling. My two sisters are very special friends, and over the years, I could not bear the thought of something happening to one of them. Each of us is unique, and yet we have the common bond of blood, genes, and family history. We sometimes have different memories even though we grew up in the same house.

"I'm not scared to die. I just don't want to die now," I said as I fought back the tears. "There's so much I still want to do, see, and complete."

Denise reached across and took my hand as she said, "Karen, you're not going to die now. The doctor got all the cancer."

I so wanted to believe her, just as I wanted to believe Jim when he said those same words. But how do we know the cancer is all gone? Who's to say it won't come back? Are they in denial of reality? Or do *I* not trust enough?

Once we exhausted talking about the "Big C," we moved to other topics, many of which brought smiles, giggles, or laughter. We left the coffee shop arm in arm, and we agreed it would be so much better if we lived closer.

Denise went to Qigong with me one morning, where she felt very welcome and at peace. "I could feel the love," she said. "I understand why you like to go there."

The last night Randy and Denise were here, we sat around the dinette table as they led us in communion. They lit a candle and placed it in the middle of the table. From the Bible they read Luke 22:14–20, broke some pieces of bread on a plate, and filled our glasses with juice. They took turns reading the passages as they moved slowly around the table and placed their hands on Jim and me. It was a beautiful time, and the room was filled with love. My tears were not of sadness or fear, but of the overwhelming joy only God can provide.

We can turn our backs on tomorrow
And live for yesterday.
Or we can be happy for tomorrow
Because of yesterday.

—Anonymous

Chapter 16

Celebrating Life

I saw Dr. Boente before my fourth chemotherapy. He was surprised when I said I felt fine. Jim corroborated that I was as full of energy as ever.

"Well, your white count is too low, and it would be dangerous to give you the chemotherapy today," Dr. Boente said. "We will postpone it for a week to give you time to build your white count back up."

I actually felt disappointed that I would not get my chemotherapy. Even though a low white blood cell count is a common side effect of chemotherapy, I felt a sense of failure that my body had not withstood the trauma of chemo. I had hoped all the good nutrition, exercise, and prayer would eliminate chemo's effects on my noncancerous cells. Perhaps I was feeling good, despite the low white cell count, because of those very healthy factors.

"There is an injection called Neulasta, which you'll receive the day after your chemo treatment," Dr. Boente explained. "It'll help prevent the decrease in your white count. It's an expensive, but very effective, medication that costs around $6,000 per injection." Dr. Boente smiled as Jim and I looked at each other in shock. He continued, "Fortunately, Medicare does pay for it."

This drug can have some severe side effects, primarily of nausea, bone pain, and headaches for about 50 percent of the patients. Dr. Boente instructed me to take Claritin for one week after the injection, since it appeared to eliminate or decrease the severity of the side effects for about 75 percent of the people suffering from them.

Some nights were difficult, as I had enough joint pain in my right knee either to keep me awake or wake me out of a sound sleep. I was concerned about this new medication, Neulasta, but I also knew I must take it if I were to continue chemotherapy. Fortunately, I did not suffer with any headaches or nausea.

My ability to remember and comprehend was worse than ever. I mentioned it to Dr. Boente's nurse, and that was when I first learned about "chemo brain," which is a well-documented phenomenon. My mind just could not remember or comprehend well. I was unable to read a book or a newspaper and then remember what I had just read. Jim was very kind and patient, helping me retain, remember, or understand information, especially from Dr. Boente or any of the medical staff. Dr. Boente assured me that once I completed chemotherapy, these mental symptoms would disappear, and I would be back to normal.

I had always taken pride in the health of my body, and I believed I had taken very good care of it for the past sixty-seven years. I had always been physically active through sports, exercising, dance, and golf. Only for a short time, I smoked cigarettes in college to be cool. I only socially drank wine, always took vitamins and supplements, and ate nutritiously. I practiced prayer, meditation, and positive thinking for my spiritual and mental health. But now I had all these drugs entering my system to either destroy cancer cells or treat side effects. Would my otherwise strong and healthy body be able to withstand the negative effects of chemotherapy? For me, the answer was to continue living, eating, praying, and thinking as I had all my life.

I met with the clinic's nutritionist, who gave me the following advice: "Eat yogurt every day. Buy organic, not Yoplait or Dannon, for the most probiotics, which help with the immune system and bowels." She also instructed, "Pumpkin seeds are high in fiber and antioxidants, and just two Brazil nuts a day will meet your minimum daily requirement for selenium." She encouraged me to start doing yoga again, as well as continue my daily walks.

At one of the Qigong classes, I learned about the benefits of black sesame seed tea. These seeds are very beneficial to the kidney meridian, which is the master meridian that can be so easily depleted during an illness. I asked Dr. Boente if it were okay to drink this tea. He smiled and said, "That's fine."

✣

Jim and I talked about joining some kind of support group to help us through each phase of the journey. I did not want our lives to be all about cancer and to have every decision ruled by the status of my health. I didn't want me or my life to be such a roller coaster of emotions. The clinic offered support groups, which we agreed we would explore in the near future. I knew talking to other people could be very helpful, but it was important that the group be uplifting and educational. Neither of us wanted to be subjected to negativity.

I continued to go to Qigong every week and meditated almost every day with the Christ Spirit guiding my prayers. I tried to incorporate some aspect of positive thinking, breathing exercises, imagery, or prayer into every minute of my daily life.

> *The more you praise and celebrate your life,*
> *The more there is in life to celebrate.*
>
> —Oprah Winfrey

Chapter 17

Keep Fighting

Our son, Richard, along with his wife, Amy, and their two sons flew in for a five-day visit from Mesa, Arizona. It was our first time to see each other since my surgery, though we had talked on the telephone several times a week.

Jim and I had wonderful talks with Richard and Amy about my prognosis, my journey so far, and the effect my cancer had on everyone. He and his family share a strong faith in God and base their lives on prayer and scripture. At first, my grandsons looked at me with wide eyes when I briefly removed my hat, but then they quickly went on with their game and responded to me with unconditional love and acceptance. We all could learn from young children who have not yet learned to be prejudiced or mean to people different from them.

Richard went with Jim and me to see Dr. Boente before my fifth chemo treatment. He was very impressed with Dr. Boente, appreciating his frankness and openness as he explained my cancer and treatment thus far. I showed him the chemotherapy room, which had only a few patients at the time. It was important for me to have Richard see the chemo room, personally ask Dr. Boente questions, and be physically present in the clinic. I knew it was equally important for him.

Due to job commitments, Richard was able to stay for only three days. Jim drove him to the airport while I received my chemotherapy. It was hard to see him go, but happily, Amy and the children were staying a few extra days.

"Mom, it was hard to see you, but you look so much better than I expected," he later said after he returned to Mesa.

❧

Less than a week after the chemotherapy and Richard's visit, there were days of storm clouds in my psyche, body, and spirit. I did not sleep well for four nights in a row, due to the joint pain in both legs. I was incontinent of some urine during the night because I couldn't get out of bed quickly enough. Tears of doubt and fear were flowing like the rain during a storm. It was pity-party time, as I whined to Jim about having to take all the pills, having to be constantly aware of my bowels and bladder, having to apply makeup to my plain face, and having to constantly wear something over my bald head (even though it was totally my choice). I looked at my body that had once been so healthy and trim with some muscular definition. Now all I saw was the long scar down my flabby abdomen, the loss of muscle tone in my arms and legs, and my ashen skin. My eyebrows and eyelashes were now completely gone, too. It was hard to wake up in the morning and know Jim would see me looking like E. T. I tried to pencil in my eyebrows and eyelids right away each morning. I knew Jim didn't care, but I wanted to be as beautiful for him as I could. Losing my eyelashes and eyebrows was more devastating than my bald head, so every time I looked in the mirror, I needed to say affirmations of love to myself. I told God I would be okay if I never grew hair back anywhere on my body, so long as I could have my life. Definitely, my life was the most important thing. But despite the affirmations, I still couldn't chase every storm cloud away.

Jim put his arms around me. "Every day, every moment I have with you is a gift I treasure," he said. I looked into his eyes and whispered, "Thank you." Each day is truly a gift. Instead of thanking God only for the day I just experienced, I needed to thank God for the day I was about to live—and pray that I would live it as He would have me. When a person receives a gift, they must thank the giver and then enjoy the gift.

The moral of those stormy days was to live each day fully with love, do what I believed to be good and healthy for my body, and not worry about tomorrow. Symbolically, I put on my dancing shoes and danced. I could let it rain, snow, storm, or shine. It really did not matter, as long as I had that day.

> *I must work the works of Him while it is light, for the*
> *night cometh when no man can work.*
> —John 9:4, *Good News Bible*

Chapter 18

The Gift of Friends

In mid-October, I had a wonderful two-hour lunch with five friends I have known for forty years. We first met when I moved to Waconia, Minnesota. It felt like just yesterday since we had last seen each other, even though it had been as many as twenty years for some of them. All of us are now retired. Our friendship is strong, and we respect each other's opinions and have honest discussions.

In the years since we had last seen each other, two of our friends had become widows, one had had several serious health issues, two were struggling with husbands who had become dependent on them, and one had her daughter and grandchildren living with her.

At one point, Arlene asked me how I managed such a positive attitude about my cancer and the chemotherapy. I replied that I have great faith in God, my doctor, the support and prayers of my family and friends, and meditation and healing energy. As she hugged me, she whispered in my ear, "You are an inspiration to me."

"Your hair will grow back," "You're going to be fine," and "I know God will watch over you" are statements from one friend who survived throat cancer. She shared how so much of her strength came not only from her faith in God, but also from the support of people around her. Like me, she saw the miracle of people's kindness and compassion as they reached out to her with everything from cards to casseroles to cleaning.

During this lunch, we shared laughter, stories, sadness, and concerns. We looked each other in the eye, placed a hand on a shoulder, smiled, and hugged. No one goes through this life without some challenges. We would be selfish to say, "Why me?" instead of "Why *not* me?" It's true that God will not give us more than we can handle. When my hours or days were the toughest, it was often a friend who helped me.

True friendships survive despite distance and time, financial differences, or marital changes from divorce or death. A friendship requires unconditional love, which means each friend celebrates the positive changes as well as challenges the negative changes in the other. Jealousy, greed, selfishness, and abuse cannot be part of a friendship, as each of these negative and harmful qualities is destructive to the recipient as well as the giver.

These wonderful women gave me a blanket they had made by each putting their talent to use. They gather together once a week to make such blankets, pray, and read scripture. They are doing the ministry of God.

> *Within every person is a light that radiates wisdom, love, peace, life, and goodness. This light is the light of Christ.*
>
> —Peggy Pifer

Chapter 19

An Ending and a New Beginning

On November 3, I attended Qigong for the last time until May, when we would return from our annual six months of living in Florida. Our small group seemed even more cohesive, or was it just me? The meditation that day was for healing those with cancer and those who love them. At the end of class, the leader asked everyone to stand in a circle around me while I sat in a chair. Each of them was instructed to send love to me, singing my name in whatever tune or melody they chose. It was a beautiful and uplifting experience that I carry with me every day. It's such a wonderful gift when people send love out to anyone. Love is an umbrella when the storms of life seem overwhelming.

Three days later, I went to see Dr. Boente and have what I hoped would be my last chemotherapy session. He said that since my CA125 results had consistently been in the single-digit range, he would not prescribe any more chemotherapy. He encouraged us to live as we always had before, which meant we could return to Florida for the winter. He referred me to Dr. Holloway, a gynecological oncologist in Orlando. I was relieved and happy. For the first time, I felt more like a survivor.

☙

I prayed my journey with active cancer was now over. I know I will always have the "Big C" sitting on my shoulders, whispering in my ears with every little change or feeling in my body and with every doctor's appointment and lab test. I made a commitment to keep positive thoughts and energy around me, do my daily prayers and meditations, take vitamins and minerals high in antioxidants, eat nutritiously, and exercise wisely. I have always loved yoga, and the dietician recommended I start doing it again for its physical, mental, emotional, and spiritual benefits.

I felt very good about my decision to have chemotherapy and also incorporate complementary treatments. The chemo was like lightning: It had good qualities in how it burned away cancer cells, giving new light to the body. However, lightning can also strike and burn trees or buildings, just as chemo can burn healthy cells. I was fortunate that my side effects were relatively mild, which allowed me to tolerate chemo. For some people, only natural, alternative treatments may be right for them.

The six chemotherapy sessions had been like going through thunderstorms. The first treatment was so new, foreign, and scary, but each subsequent one was easier because I was familiar with the process. Just like holding a small child's hand during a thunderstorm, the nurses held my hand in a symbolic way with their kind faces, reassuring smiles, and informative answers to my questions.

Even though I had completed the prescribed chemotherapy treatments, I continued to go through the various stages of grief, staying in each one for different periods of time. The stages of grief are not linear or predictable. A person might go from one stage to another, then back to the original stage. I knew remaining in the stage of acceptance was the healthiest.

Look to this day for it is the very day of Life
In its brief course lie all the verities and realities
    of your existence.
For yesterday is but a dream
And tomorrow is only a vision
But today well-lived makes every yesterday
    a dream of Happiness
Look well, therefore, to this day,
It is the life of Life.
                    —Sanskrit

PHASE IV

Healing Anew

Chapter 20

Healing after Chemo

After I completed chemotherapy, it was my time to declare victory over cancer. I won the battle, and only time would tell if I won the war. I felt great, though I still struggled with some occasional incontinence and constipation. I wore pads to catch any unexpected leaks and made sure I emptied my bladder before venturing out. High fiber and lots of water or juice were part of my daily diet.

We left for Florida on November 13, eager to leave the cold Minnesota weather behind us. We arrived three days later, and our Florida neighbors and friends greeted us with big smiles, hugs, and words of how great I looked. It was good to be out gardening and playing golf, and I was proactive with applying sunscreen on every exposed area of skin. There were lots of weeds to pull, mulch to apply, and annuals to plant. I played golf one or two times a week. (The plus side of not being a great golfer is that all that swinging is great exercise!) My spirits were up, but I still worried what the results of my next PET scan in March might be.

Due to the illness of cancer and the side effects of chemotherapy, I had adopted certain daily actions that I continued in Florida. I still needed to build up my immune system, so I was very concerned about contracting any cold or flu. I avoided small children, crowds, and cigarette smoke. I washed my hands more often—almost obsessively. In the doctor's office, I'd sit at a distance from people. In restaurants, I would ask for tables away from other people. One time, I moved to a different table in a coffee shop when a young lady near me was sneezing and blowing her nose, even though she was telling her companion how bad her allergies had been.

As always, I got my seasonal flu shot and took vitamin C tablets daily. If I felt even the slightest warning signs of a cold, I took three tablets of Wellness Formula supplements every three hours until the symptoms were gone. This amazing supplement contains high doses of vitamins C and A, plus such natural ingredients such as garlic, elderberry, and echinacea, which promote the immune system.

We attended a cancer support group in our town of Tavares, Florida, in early February, just three months after my last chemotherapy. We decided to go for two reasons. One was to find out if that group would provide some of the support I was missing at the time. I felt somewhat isolated away from Dr. Boente, his staff, my family, and the weekly Qigong gatherings back in Minnesota.

The other reason was that I had read in the newspaper that the group was featuring a special speaker—a registered nurse who was a breast cancer survivor. Her presentation was on the topic of surviving cancer and described the time from diagnosis through the rest of the person's life. She listed eight characteristics of a survivor personality: strong spiritual belief, strong support system, sense of humor, connection to nature, goals, good nutrition, regular exercise, and openness to new experiences. I found her words inspirational and reassuring.

> *When you talk about healing, you're including the way you live your life.*
> —Dawna Markova

Chapter 21

The Loving Husband

I had awakened to a beautiful Florida "winter" morning, when suddenly an unexpected storm hit me. My self-esteem was being challenged. My hair was growing back, but it was too much and in areas of my body where there had never been hair before—my hands, fingers, and face. The hair on my head was about a half inch long, and it was the same color as before, but it appeared to have some curl now. People encouraged me to go without a hat or scarf because they thought my hairstyle was cute and stylish. They told me I looked great, but I didn't think so. My ego was getting in the way.

Jim said something to me about the hair on my face, and it made me feel so hurt and angry, I couldn't speak to him. I knew he didn't say it to hurt me, but that didn't change the way I felt. I felt twisted and torn up inside. I was of course thankful to be alive, but I still couldn't help but struggle to feel good about myself and accept the reality of how I looked. I knew love is blind and it's not how a person looks that matters. The flip side of it, though, is the truth of how our society judges beauty. Once again, my own vanity was being tested.

Later on, I apologized to Jim for overreacting to his statement about the hair on my face. He shared that he hadn't meant facial hair, but the hair on my head. "Your hair in front and around your ears is sticking out, and I think it looks cute," he said. "Let me show you." We went to the bathroom mirror, and I had to agree with him.

We talked about how each of us had adjusted to each new day's adventure since my cancer was diagnosed in June of the previous year. Now while my body was recovering, I had new growth of hair, a change in appetite and bowel habits, skin changes, and energy fluctuations. We were so truly thankful for each minute and day we had together, and with that, we smiled and gave thanks to God.

⟡

One of the consequences of not only a hysterectomy but also chemotherapy is the loss of the libido. I had no sex drive at all. I didn't fantasize about it or miss it. Sometimes I smiled with happiness as I recalled the wonderful romantic and sexual times, but soon tears followed. Jim and I talked about it, and he was understanding and kind. I dedicate the following story to my loving husband, Jim, who has given me the same love this gentleman gave his wife.

> It was a busy morning, about 8:30, when an elderly gentleman in his 80's arrived at the clinic where I work as an RN. He had to have stitches removed from his thumb. He said he was in a hurry as he had an appointment at 9:00 am.
>
> I took his vital signs and had him take a seat, knowing it be over an hour before someone would be able to see him.
>
> I saw him looking at his watch and decided since I was not busy with another patient I would evaluate his wound.
>
> On exam, it was well healed so I talked to one of the doctors, got the needed supplies to remove his sutures and redress his wound.

While taking care of his wound, I asked him if he had another doctor's appointment this morning, as he was in such a hurry. The gentleman told me no, that he needed to go to the nursing home to eat breakfast with his wife.

I asked about her health. He told me that she had been there for a while and that she was a victim of Alzheimer's disease. As we talked, I asked if she would be upset if he was a bit late. He replied that she no longer knew who he was, that she had not recognized him for five years now.

I was surprised, and asked him, "And you still go every morning even though she doesn't know who you are?"

He smiled as he patted my hand and said, "She doesn't know me but I still know who she is."

I had to hold back tears as he left. I had goose bumps on my arm and thought, "That is the kind of love I want in my life."

True love is neither physical nor romantic. True love is an acceptance of all that is, has been, will be, and will not be.

The happiest people don't necessarily have the best of everything; they just make the best of everything they have.

We all want to receive this kind of love, but somehow, I think, the better part is to be in a position to give this kind of love.

—Author unknown

Chapter 22

Learning from Others

During those first few months in Florida, I learned some big lessons from compete strangers. It was another example of how people come into our lives to teach us something.

As I sat in a coffee shop one morning the first week of March, I read about a young British actress who had terminal cancer and had just married the love of her life a few days earlier. Though she was only in her twenties, she had taken on the incredible challenge of her illness with a maturity and determination few of us have at any age. She was living each minute to its fullest, which is what each of us needs to do. In her white wedding gown on her special day, she beamed with great joy, proudly displaying her beautiful bald head. I asked myself, "Could I do that?"

Her story reminded me of an article I had read in the *Orlando Sentinel* back in January about seventeen-year-old Jenny Curovic, who was diagnosed with Stage IV ovarian cancer. She had complained of abdominal pain and passed out while playing at her junior-varsity basketball game. She had a twenty-inch cancerous tumor on an ovary. She had no family history of ovarian cancer, and except for some occasional stomach cramps, she had been symptom free until that night of the basketball game. Even when the cancer had spread to one lung, Jenny remained an optimist and a fighter. She kept herself laughing and smiling by watching the *Fantastic Four* over and over. She competed with her sister on a surfboard while on a trip to Hawaii sponsored by the Make-A-Wish Foundation. One month after her last chemo treatment, she was back on the court, shooting basketballs.

Ovarian cancer can strike any woman at any age, even an athletic young teen. Jenny's attitude and determination to be victorious over her battle with cancer—as well as the aggressive chemotherapy prescribed by her oncologist—contributed to her now being cancer free. Jenny Curovic is a role model for us all.

As I sat there drinking my chai tea in Starbucks, I was wearing my white hat over my three-quarter-inch hair. I observed a girl in her late teens who was wearing torn jeans, flip-flops showing dirty feet, and a white spaghetti-strap top that did not cover her fat belly. Yes, I used the word *fat*. I obviously didn't know how much she weighed, but she must have been about seventy-five pounds overweight. I thought, *I would never dress in torn clothes, expose dirty feet, and accentuate a part of my body that even I knew was too fat.* How was I doing for judging?

But the young girl was obviously happy or proud of how she looked, or she did not care how others thought of her. I then knew I had a lesson to learn from her. How many times did God have to show me what Athena, Janice, and the British actress already knew? Was I, with my lack of a full head of hair, any different from someone on crutches, in a wheelchair, or dragging a leg and holding an arm in an awkward position after a stroke? What about those who suffer from depression and walk with downcast eyes, slumped shoulders, and dark clouds surrounding their overburdened bodies? So I *had* cancer! I was still alive, and I needed to be proud of my very short hairstyle. It was a testament to what I went through to fight this disease.

I took my last swallow of the chai tea, then removed my hat and let the cool air of the air conditioner blow gently on my head. Guess what? The earth did not stop revolving, and no one stared at me. I put away my computer, gathered my belongings, and walked out of Starbucks without noticing anyone looking at me in any particular way.

What a great lesson to learn, and hopefully it freed me to be a role model for others. It's not how we look, but how true we are to our souls that matters. Perhaps the young girl in the torn jeans had dressed to the best of her financial ability, or maybe she had lost a lot of weight already. Who was I to judge how she dressed or looked? Thank you, God, for this young lady and for Jenny. I asked to be forgiven, and thanked God for helping me be my own beautiful *me*. I was reminded of the Serenity Prayer:

> *God, grant me the serenity to accept the things*
> *I cannot change,*
> *Courage to change the things I can,*
> *And wisdom to know the difference.*
>   —Reinhold Niebuhr

Chapter 23

Life Is to Be Lived

One day in early March, I slipped and bruised a rib under my breast while I was washing the car. It was a ridiculous accident and would never have happened if I had slowed down a little and listened to my inner voice. It was yelling at me just a nanosecond before I fell. I could have changed shoes, waited until Jim came home, ignored the dirty spot, or just found some better way to remove the unreachable spot. But no, I ignored any cautionary whispers and stood on the metal door frame with my wet shoes.

This accident happened the day before my sixty-eighth birthday, when some close friends were coming to celebrate the next evening. I was determined to not let this mishap stop me from having fun, so I went ahead with my plans, ignoring the pain as much as I could. We played games, ate wonderful food, laughed, and talked. No one except Jim was wise to my extreme discomfort.

For the next week, I nursed my sore rib with rest, heat, and an occasional Advil. By the following week, I was able to swing the golf club without pain, so I played nine holes, getting one of my best scores. However, I did find that bending over to get my ball out of the hole, pick up extra clubs, or place my tee in the ground quickly began to irritate my rib. By the time I got home, I was miserable. I paid the price for the next four days, which brought me back to the lesson God was trying to teach me: I needed to learn how to slow down, keep my mind uncluttered, and listen more to my body and inner voice.

Ten days after my unfortunate carwash accident, I had my first appointment with Dr. Robert Holloway, the oncologist in

Orlando Dr. Boente had recommended. First I had a PET/CT scan across the street from Dr. Holloway's office. Combining the two scans has proven to give more valuable information than they provide as separate scans. This was my first time to have the combined scans, and though it was a longer process, it wasn't any more uncomfortable or frightening. I did feel like a mummy— they had me so wrapped up and strapped down, I couldn't have moved if I wanted to.

Jim and I both liked Dr. Holloway immediately. He was personable, warm, and willing to answer questions from my ever-present purple notebook. My CA125 was at 7.0, and my scans were normal—except for some evidence of a healed small rib fracture! Jim and I celebrated the good news with a lunch at the White Wolf Café just a few blocks away.

❧

I've always been an energetic and active person, having many projects at one time. That's all good and well, except when I put too much stress on my mind and body, such as with the rib accident. Since my cancer diagnosis, I've felt an urgency to pack a lot into each day, even each minute. I've worried whether I will get everything done before I leave this earth. But I'm sure I could live to be two hundred years old and still not have everything done, because I seem to always find new projects to complete and new interests to explore and experience.

I've been organizing family photos, making albums for each child and grandchild. I've also been putting together a family history, taking advantage of Ancestry.com, and writing personal antidotes I recall about grandparents, aunts, uncles, and parents. Someday soon I want to get all my recipes in order and create

Oma's Treasury of Recipes. I truly believe I could pick one recipe a day and still not use all the recipes I've accumulated over the years.

I've written one novel and haven't even tried to get it published. I also have a second book that's only partly done on paper, though I have the story completed in my head. I believe a novel tells more about an author than perhaps a sculpture or painting reveals about an artist. I feel comfortable sharing some of my poetry, but I have a greater fear and resistance when it comes to sharing my novels. Perhaps I worry the reader will learn something about me I do not want revealed.

From the illness of cancer to the injury of my rib, I've learned the value of living each day fully with great appreciation. Living fully does not mean cramming every minute with activity or busy thoughts, but living it with peace, fulfillment, and joy while doing the things God wants me to do. So when I think I cannot handle one more problem, like the accident with my rib, I need only to remember it's an opportunity to learn about myself, make some positive changes, and hopefully use the lesson to help others.

I find there are those moments of peace, quiet eddies,
when I feel again the Joy—like warm rays from
the sun.
—John W. Sheppard

Chapter 24

People Reach Out

Since I began this journey, I've been amazed by how many
people have had cancer and willingly talked about their illnesses
with me. Whether in Minnesota or Florida, I experienced this
many times at support groups, in private conversations with
friends or acquaintances, or even with strangers.

A few weeks after my surgery that past June, Angela, a
neighbor in Minnesota, shared her experiences of battling cancer
since she was nineteen years old during the days of cobalt radiation. She still suffers with the side effects, but is cancer free. She
radiantly smiles and says, "God is good. There were times when
the doctors were not sure I would live, let alone ever get pregnant.
Well, here I am." She is the mother of three healthy young men.
Angela and her husband pray together every morning. What a
beautiful way to start the day.

Once we returned to Florida, I experienced more special
moments with people who had been touched by cancer. Even
though the weather was warm, I was often still feeling cold—
one of the side effects of chemotherapy. A saleslady in a city
nearby helped me pick out two cardigans, perfect in style, size,
color, and price. She shared that she had had breast cancer ten
years ago and remembered feeling chilled, also. She handed me
my package of new sweaters, then hugged me and said, "You're
going to be okay."

One day I was in Lowe's, looking at all the beautiful flowers,
trying to decide which ones I would buy for our Florida front
yard. While I stood admiring the purple petunias, a woman

came up to me and said, "I love your hair. Where do you get it cut? I want mine to look just like yours."

By this time, my hair was about one and a half inches long, and it was showing some early signs of curls. I smiled, placed my hand on her arm, and said, "Oh, thank you, but I had cancer, and this is my first growth of hair since chemotherapy."

The woman was genuinely surprised and saddened. "I'm so sorry," she said. She then quickly added, "You're going to be all right. I just know you will." I smiled and thanked her.

I thought our conversation was over, but she said, "You know, you look just like Jamie Lee Curtis." I had heard those very words from others, so again I thanked her for such a nice compliment. Then she took me by complete surprise when she added, "But you could use a facelift."

After the initial shock, I laughed and said, "I'm sure I would benefit from a facelift, but at my age, whom would I be kidding?"

The now-embarrassed woman replied, "Oh, I'm sure I'm much older than you."

"Well, I'm sixty-eight years old, and these wrinkles and sags are just part of my age," I laughed, trying to ease her obvious discomfort.

She held her hands up to her face and said, "My goodness—I'm sixty, and you look much younger than me!" We both laughed and bid goodbye. Her last words were, "Good luck to you. I'll pray for you, but I know you'll be okay."

I have shared this story with many people, because it demonstrates several wonderful things about human beings and life. First of all, it's proof that no matter how we may feel about our appearance, there's at least one person (and probably many more) who likes our "look." On a deeper level, it's so good to appreciate our chronological age; accept how our bodies show our age, health, and disposition; and otherwise acknowledge our genuine selves.

Second is the lesson that what we say may not always come out the way we intended. It creates an opportunity for the receiver to bring comfort to an awkward or embarrassing time with smiling and laughing rather than with defensiveness or anger. Sometimes what seems like an insult is actually a compliment that just came out the wrong way.

I wonder if this kind lady has remembered our encounter or shared it with other people. Did she come away from our meeting any stronger, happier, or enriched? She touched my life in a very special and dear way. Each time I share this story, I hope others learn something beneficial from it.

In contrast to the people with whom I have shared positive moments during my journey, other people are not so comfortable being around someone who has or had the "Big C." Were they afraid they might get cancer from me? Did I bring up painful memories of others they knew who had had cancer? Did they just not want to be reminded of their own mortality? One special person in my life has not been able to cry or pray with me during my journey, even though I yearn for such a relationship. At times, she can be negative and self-absorbed, so I haven't always wanted to be around her. I hope one day she'll be able to nurture herself so she can nurture others.

We don't always realize the impact our words or actions might have on someone. My grandmother taught me the importance of always trying to reach out to others with a smile, kind word, or helping hand. How often do we let opportunities of kindness pass us by on airplanes, in restaurants, in stores, in traffic, or wherever? Glancing away from someone with a physical image different from the norm can be hurtful, but a smile can warm any heart. The power of making a difference in someone's life is a lesson to be well learned.

> I saw a young man walking up and down a beach after the tide had gone out.
>
> The young man would pick up a starfish, left behind by the tide, and would throw it as far as he could back into the ocean.
>
> "What are you trying to do?" I asked.
>
> "Make a difference," he replied.
>
> "But the beach is covered with starfish! You can't possibly expect to make a difference for them all!" I stated.
>
> As he picked up another starfish and threw it into the ocean, he replied, "I made a difference for that one."
>
> —Adapted from "The Star Thrower" by Loren Eiseley

Chapter 25

Spirituality

As I continued to recover from my battle with cancer, I gained my strength because I knew God was beside me and because I'll always have His shoulders to lean upon. I do not believe God *gave* me cancer, but He allowed it to happen, and He responded to prayers in accordance with what was best for me. I believe we always have lessons to learn, and that's what life's experiences are about. If we don't learn our lessons the first time, then life will keep bringing us new opportunities to learn. In the Bible, the story of Job illustrates this so well.

My daily prayer was—and will continue to be—that my body will be cancer free for that day and that I will live that day as God wants me to. Did I some days get caught up in the importance of material things, envy someone else's success or health, worry about mundane things, or have my own pity party? You bet I did! But I was also more aware than ever that each day was a beautiful gift.

Deep daily meditation was very helpful during the healing process, as it always brought me back to center with God right there in my core. For me, meditation is a deep state of relaxation and quietness, which allows my soul to be uncluttered by the thoughts and distractions of the conscious mind. Whenever I turned to meditation during my journey, I always started with a prayer asking for the Christ Spirit to guide and surround me, because I didn't want any other influences to take advantage of me. Then I listened to a meditation tape or just some beautiful, soothing music, which helped quiet my conscious mind.

Everything I have ever read or learned about meditation has said that learning to quiet the conscious mind is the most difficult thing, because it's used to being in control. Sometimes I suddenly found myself thinking about extraneous things.

In addition to meditation, I also turned to prayer, which were special words I said out loud or silently throughout the day. I said familiar, established prayers, such as grace before a meal. But I also said spontaneous words of thanks for certain blessings, for the courage to face certain situations, or for clarity of mind to gain certain knowledge. These words from well-known prayers were very powerful for me:

Thy will be done

The Lord is my Shepherd

God is great

My soul to keep

Forgive us our debts

Come, Lord Jesus

By still waters

PHASE V

Looking Back

Chapter 26

Remission

We returned to Minnesota in May after a wonderful winter in Florida. As I approached my first year of being cancer free, I felt anxious about my upcoming doctor's appointment. Tears were flowing for my fear of the unknown, or I swallowed them as I tried to hide my true emotions. Jim saw through me and said, "Together we will face whatever lies ahead—good news or not." I felt better when I heard his words.

Fear is an interesting phenomenon that can either motivate you or hold you in a state of inaction—or worse, put you in a state of total immobility. For example, the fear of an attack can make your adrenaline flow with full force to give you the strength, endurance, and courage to either fight the assailant or run in flight. But fear of the unknown can often lead to depression as a person spirals down, due to his or her inability to cope. Once they identify the "unknown," many people are able to face their challenge with courage, while others may become more depressed. In my opinion, people who spiral down even more may not have a firm foundation of faith, may not have proper information and education, or may not have learned from their elders how to face life's calamities in a healthy manner.

I reread "The Litany against Fear," which I had received in a card from my cousin Farley. It comforted me. Then I picked up the telephone and called the nurse, Ann, to find out the results of my CA125 test. I figured if the level were in the normal range, she would tell me over the phone. If it were high, then she might say the results were not back yet or otherwise have me wait until

Dr. Boente could discuss it at my appointment the next day. Either way, I felt good about taking some initiative in my care.

Fortunately, Ann came right out and said my test result was wonderfully low at 7.2. I gave Jim the thumbs up signal. Once I hung up with Ann, Jim and I held each other and cried tears of gratefulness. Then we just collapsed in our chairs and talked about how thankful we were for that day, for each other, for Dr. Boente, and for living here in the United States, where one can receive such excellent care. "Now let's plan our trip to the British Isles," Jim said with a big smile on his face.

A short time later, June, the scheduler at the doctor's office called. June was one of the first people I met at the Minnesota Oncology clinic. She is less than five feet tall, a dynamo of energy, and a great listener who has full empathy with the journey I am on. She's a cancer survivor who often reassures me with statements like, "You have the best doctor in the field" and "We will do everything we can for you." She reminds me of my mother, who was 4'11" and often said, "Dynamite comes in small packages."

June asked about moving my appointment to an earlier time so I could see Molly, the physician's assistant, instead of Dr. Boente. At first I was a little alarmed and disappointed, but I quickly realized it meant Dr. Boente was confident about my health status as well as confident about Molly's ability. I agreed to the change.

When I met Molly, I was surprised at how young she appeared, but she greeted us with a big smile, good eye contact, and a hand shake. I liked her right away. She listened intently to each question from my purple notebook and either answered articulately or said, "I don't know, but I'll find out." And she did. I like people who can be honest and self-confident enough to say they don't know an answer. Molly said I didn't need a CT or PET scan because my blood level and physical exam were normal. It was such good news.

Dr. Boente came in briefly to say hello. I greeted him with a hug and thanked him for everything he had done. He said he was pleased with how well I was doing and thanked me for seeing Molly instead of him. "I have a patient in the hospital that I need to operate on as soon as possible," he said. "But she has other serious health issues, so I'm over at the hospital more than I'm here in the office today." Hearing of this patient's health made me recall Dr. Boente's words a year earlier, when he said I was very healthy—except that I had cancer.

☙

I learned some important lessons from the days around that appointment. One lesson is to be your own advocate and not be afraid to be assertive and ask questions. Another lesson is to be open to the experience of trusting someone new. In other words, I learned to trust Molly, which freed Dr. Boente's time to help another patient. Finally is the lesson to not let fear run your day or life. Face the fear and deal with it through education, prayer, and talking to other people. We are what we think. So always think positive, give the benefit of the doubt, and see the glass more than half full.

> *Love never gives up; and its faith, hope and patience never fail.*
>
> —I Corinthians 13:7, *Good News Bible*

Chapter 27

New-Birth Day

June 20 was my first new-birth day—one year to the day when I had my surgery and learned the tumor was malignant. Some people celebrate their last day of chemotherapy as the start of remission. But June 20 was the start of my new life. I was reborn.

I celebrated in a quiet way with Jim and our son, Scott, at his cabin in northern Minnesota. As Scott mowed the grass and weeds, Jim watched the U.S. Open, and I did my writing. The sky was blue, there was a gentle breeze, and I tried to hear the birds chirping over the roar of the mower and the voices on the television.

I felt so blessed to have had the last year to spend with Jim, the family, and our dear friends. I saw parts of the country I had not seen before. I learned to be more patient and understanding. I became ever closer to God. And I shared tears and laughter with so many people. Hopefully I had been able to help others through my words or actions. I planted new flowers, embroidered gifts, cleaned out closets, and gave away treasures to the kids and grandchildren. I wrote this very book and started the third rewrite of my first novel.

In my heart, I sang "Happy New-Birth Day to Me." There was no cake, ice cream, or candles. No gifts, no games. It was just a day of quiet enjoyment with people I love and with the beauty of the world I treasure. In the deepest part of me, I knew that whatever rainstorms may come my way, I will always try to let my light outshine any pain or fear.

*Wherever we are or whatever we may be doing,
the light of Christ shines within us.*

—Peggy Pifer

Epilogue

As I write this, I have celebrated three years of being cancer free. In some respects, these past few years have been more difficult than the five months of surgery and active treatment.

I see either Dr. Boente in Minnesota or Dr. Holloway in Florida every six months for a physical exam and the CA125 blood draw. But for the first two years after completing my chemotherapy, I saw a doctor every three months. So, I was scared when Dr. Holloway said, "We'll now start seeing you every six months." The thought of going such a long time without a blood test or exam was truly frightening. "You'll be fine," he reassured me. "If you have any symptoms or concerns, just call, and we'll check you."

To this day, I feel like a large log is lifted off my shoulders after each appointment. This sense of relief lasts until two to three weeks before my next appointment, when fear and worry creep up and weigh me down again. I know each day that goes by without a reoccurrence of the cancer decreases the likelihood of it ever coming back. But still, in talking with other survivors, my reactions are not at all unusual.

I know fear is the basis for this anxiety. It's not fear of dying, as I have a strong belief and peace in the journey after I leave this life. It's fear of not living long enough to see my grandchildren become young adults, marry, and have their own children. I want to finish some of my many projects, and most important, I want to spend more time with my husband and family. I know no one knows when his or her earthly life will come to an end, so I fill my days by appreciating the beauty of the world around me, enjoying activities that are fulfilling, and spending quality time with people.

This increased anxiety I experience as a cancer survivor decreases in intensity if I use the same coping mechanisms that first saw me through the diagnosis, surgery, and treatment. My faith in God is the foundation for all the other ways I deal with being a survivor. In addition, Jim continues to be a solid rock who's always here for me. I continue to do Qigong, exercise with our new Wii set, use sunscreen liberally, take vitamins and minerals, and be conscientious about my diet.

Jim and I also attend two support groups once a month in Florida. One group meets once a month at an Orlando restaurant. The second group is called the Bodacious Ovarian Diva Survivors (BODS). They meet every other month at one of the members' homes or at a restaurant. Both groups are for fellowship and support. Each woman has a unique journey to share, and they all inspire me with their faith, knowledge, and attitude. They come with wigs, turbans, or hats, and some have their natural hair back. Some are twelve- to-fifteen-year survivors, while others are in the beginning steps of survival with their first rounds of chemotherapy. We are of all ages, sizes, and races. The spouses or caregivers are inspirational, too, with their strength, love, and support as they share about their own journeys. There's always a lot of healing laughter while we share stories about *us*, not just the cancer that affected each of us.

Having gone through this journey myself, I'm now more aware of the needs of those receiving chemotherapy, so I've been knitting afghans, shawls, hats, and scarves. Other women have donated their knitted, crocheted, or quilted items along with mine, which I then take to different chemotherapy sites. I'm also now more sensitive to women I see with their bandanas, hats, or bald heads. I look them in the eyes, smile, and offer some kind of a greeting.

One woman in line at our local post office was dressed in pink shorts, had a pink ribbon on her collar, and a pink hat over her bald head. She was standing with fear emanating from her body, and her eyes were like a deer's caught in headlights.

I asked, "Are you a cancer survivor?"

"I don't know," she replied in a shaky voice.

"Yes, you are a survivor," I said. "You are here today. I'm a survivor, and so are you." At that point, she smiled slightly as her husband put his arm around her.

❧

Being a survivor also makes me more aware of and grateful for the women and men who make a difference in the battle with ovarian cancer. I honor those physicians who are confident and assertive enough to refer a woman to a gynecological oncologist for evaluation of possible cancer symptoms, however remote the symptoms might appear. I honor, too, the researchers working hard to learn more about the disease. I'm encouraged with the new research showing HE4 as a more reliable marker than CA125 for epithelial ovarian cancer. Early research suggests HE4 could be especially helpful in screening ovarian cancer at its early—and most treatable—stages. There's also research on vaccines that brings new hope for women in remission. Some vaccines are currently being tested in clinical trials. I'm also grateful for people like Liz Tilberis, who as president of the Ovarian Cancer Research Fund did so much to promote its cause. Unfortunately, she made her passing from this life in 1999, just six years after her diagnosis.

From my own experiences, I applaud those who work so diligently to raise awareness about ovarian cancer as volunteers or paid staff of the many foundations and organizations. I have met many at functions in Florida and Minnesota. I have also received encouragement, information, and inspiration from the women with ovarian cancer whom I have met at lunches, meetings, or in doctors' offices. I admire and look up to the women who have fought each battle with dignity and resourcefulness. I have learned something from each of them. Unfortunately, some have passed on, but their influence on me remains.

I met a young lady (whom I will call Lisa) at a recent Walk/ Run for Ovarian Cancer whose sister died of ovarian cancer at the age of fifty-one. Her sister was a runner, slim and petite, and she took good care of her family. There was no breast or ovarian cancer in their family. Since her sister's diagnosis, Lisa insists on getting the CA125 at her annual exams. Her physician was hesitant at first, but then responded positively to Lisa's plea, and her insurance did pay for the lab test. Lisa said she does everything she can to raise awareness to women she meets or knows. We all need to do the same.

৩

My journey with ovarian cancer has had its valleys and mountaintops, its darknesses and rays of sunshine. I do not know why I got cancer, nor do I know what the future holds for me. But what I do know is that I have learned a lot about myself these past three years, and I am a better person today than I was yesterday. I value the information I have learned about ovarian cancer and hope that I can now help others.

Appendix

Ovarian Cancer Warning Signs

1. Pelvic or abdominal pain or discomfort.

2. Vague but persistent gastrointestinal gas, nausea, and indigestion.

3. Frequent, urgent urination without infection.

4. Unexplained weight loss or gain.

5. Pelvic and abdominal swelling, bloating, or feeling of fullness.

6. Ongoing, unusual fatigue.

7. Unexplained change in bowel habits.

8. Painful intercourse.

Ovarian Cancer Risk Factors

1. Inherited mutations of *BRCA1* and *BRCA2* genes: With a mutation in one of the two genes, there is a 27 to 44 percent chance of developing ovarian cancer by age seventy.

2. Family history of ovarian cancer: The risk increases by 10 to 15 percent.

3. Family history of breast and colorectal cancers.

4. Age: Risk increases with age through the late seventies. However, it does occur in premenopausal women, too, with a peak incidence at about age fifty-nine.

5. Never having been pregnant: The more pregnancies a woman has, the less risk. Use of oral contraceptives also appears to offer some protection.

6. Infertility: Studies do show an increased risk, though the connection is not fully understood.

7. Ashkenazi Jewish descent: Mutations of *BRCA1* and *BRCA2* account for approximately 90 percent of gene mutations identified in this Jewish population.

Discussion Points

For the Person with Cancer:

1. Share your thoughts and feelings from when you first learned of your cancer diagnosis. Have they changed over time?

2. The author shares how she appreciated support and care in the forms of listening, sharing tears, hugs, encouragement, and information. What kind of support or help would you like from your family members and friends?

3. Talk about your belief or nonbelief in a God. Does religion or spirituality play a role in your life and cancer journey? In what way?

4. Is there any type of complementary therapy you want to include in your treatment plan? Why or why not?

For Family and Friends:

1. Share your thoughts and feelings from when you learned your loved one was diagnosed with cancer.

2. Each of us is unique, and so are our needs. Describe the ways you can provide support and help to your loved one and to the other friends and family on this journey.

3. The cancer patient's primary caregiver also has needs, which can sometimes be overlooked. How can you provide support and help to the primary caregiver? If you are the primary caregiver, how can you help others help you?

4. Discuss your beliefs or nonbeliefs in a God and how that impacts or affects your response to your loved one's cancer diagnosis.

5. At the end of each chapter, the author includes a quote or favorite piece of scripture or prose. Which were most meaningful to you, and why?

Recommended Resources

Organizations

American Cancer Society

Minnesota Ovarian Cancer Alliance

National Cancer Institute

National Ovarian Cancer Coalition

Ovarian Cancer Alliance of Florida

Ovarian Cancer Research Fund

Be sure to check for cancer organizations in your state and area.

Websites

www.caringbridge.org

www.chemotherapy.com

www.curetoday.com

www.doctoroz.com

www.genetichealth.com/Breast_and_Ovarian_Cancer_Home.shtml

www.inspire.com

www.mayoclinic.com/health/ovarian-cancer/DS00293

www.myriadtests.com

www.ovarian.org

www.ovationsforthecure.org

Books

A Guide to Survivorship for Women with Ovarian Cancer by
F. J. Montz and Robert E. Bristow

*A Feather in My Wig: Ovarian Cancer Cured: Twelve
(Seventeen) Years and Going Strong* by Barbara R. Van Billiard

No Time to Die: Living with Ovarian Cancer by Liz Tilberis

*The Way of Qigong: The Art and Science of Chinese Energy
Healing* by Kenneth S. Cohen

Karen Ingalls is a retired RN and has a master's degree in human development. Besides working in hospitals, clinics, and for hospice, she also had her own nursing service called Kare 'N Touch, providing clients counseling, therapeutic massage, and biofeedback. She enjoys spending time with family and friends, as well as gardening, writing, playing golf, and spreading the word about ovarian cancer. She and her husband live in St. Paul, Minnesota and Tavares, Florida.